1,001 WAYS THE REPUBLICAN PARTY IS SCREWING THE MIDDLE CLASS

Protecting Democracy from Republicans (PDR)

---❁---

Skyhorse Publishing

This book is dedicated to the hardworking people
of the American middle class.

10 9 8 7 6 5 4 3 2 1

Library of Congress Cataloging-in-Publication Data

1,001 ways the Republican Party is screwing the middle class / Protecting Democracy from Republicans (PDR).
p. cm.
 ISBN 978-1-61608-745-6 (pbk. : alk. paper)
1. Republican Party (U.S. : 1854-) 2. United States--Politics and government--2001-2009.
3. United States--Politics and government--2009- I. Protecting Democracy from Republicans. II. Title: One thousand one ways the Republican Party is screwing the middle class.
JK2356.A16 2012
324.2734--dc23

                                                                        2012016296

Printed in China

CONTENTS

INTRODUCTION

In 2010, nurse Josephine Ross and auto engineer Rebecca Carmine adopted a son. That same year, Republicans gained control of the U.S. Senate. Fearing for their child's future, Josephine and Rebecca knew that they had to take action against the impending crisis resulting from the right-wing agenda. They started small—with a community meeting that began in their home outside of Lansing, Michigan. It soon became apparent that they were not alone in their concerns, and the group grew in numbers and support. Members took to the streets and blogosphere. As the country began to gear up for the 2012 Presidential election, the couple knew they had to take action. They became acquainted with political science and economics professor Amir Hamed, who encouraged their grassroots movement. All three knew they had to get the word out to the public and make their ideas known. The fruit of their labor is the book you currently hold in your hand. Their hope is that you will be as incensed as they were at the injustices committed against the middle class by the Republican Party throughout the years, and that the citizens of America will band together for a better and more Democratic future.

---CRSO---

By writing this book, we at Protecting Democracy from Republicans (PDR) feel that giving all Americans a chance to see the indiscretions and offenses practiced by the Republican Party on the middle class will open some eyes and improve our personal and political future. With the 2012 election so near at hand, we feel that it's our duty as concerned Americans to speak up—as Howard Beale screamed in the classic film, *Network*, "I'm mad as hell, and I'm not going to take this anymore!"

Whether infringing on our constitutional rights or lining their pockets with taxpayer's money, Republicans have a long history of abusing their power for selfish reasons. While they say that they want to create jobs and improve the economy, the steps they are taking are leading in the opposite direction. They are constantly giving us "lip service," and expecting us to blindly follow them as they continue to ruin this country.

With the help of our fellow members, we've put together 1,001 examples that show the Republican Party does not have our best interests in mind. It's time for a wake-up call against their propaganda and smooth talking, and time to show them that we know the score. We refuse to continue to buy into their lies and want to show how out of touch they are with the interests of their constituents.

We at PDR believe in fighting political rhetoric with facts and, as this book demonstrates, the GOP has a long track record of ignoring and twisting these very facts to suit their agendas, whether personal or political.

Rather than looking out for the best interests of this country, they'd rather do what's best for them and the rest of the power elite. In the meantime, the hardships being faced by the middle class are unalleviated and the majority continues to be ignored by the minority.

Our goal is that you, the reader, will pick up this book and be incensed to stand up and fight back against the right-wing tyranny that is trying to take over the country we all love so dearly. The middle class is strong in numbers, and if we can come together to fight for progress, then we can secure a better future for the generations to come.

CHAPTER ONE

TODAY'S REPUBLICAN ELITE

"All conservatives are such from personal defects. They have been effeminated by position or nature, born halt and blind, through the luxury of their parents, and can only, like invalids, act on the defensive."

—Ralph Waldo Emerson

As the presidential election starts to heat up, we at PDR are keeping our fingers crossed that the Democrats stay in power. Now these are not just silly reasons, such as admiring a President who watches and plays basketball, but they are for more selfish reasons. While it is known that the state of the economy hasn't been the best in the past few years, from what the other side is saying, we see only tragedy for the middle class if they were to get elected. With the democrats staying in power, we know that the people in charge will have our best interests in mind. They will continue to look out for us and try to better the American people, especially from a financial standpoint. Included in this chapter are words of fear from the possible future leaders of this country. By the time this book is published some of the candidates may be out of the running, but that doesn't mean that they're the only ones who believe in what they say… remember that these guys all play for the same team. The problem is that these millionaires (and they are all millionaires) don't care about the middle class. They may be going to small towns across the country, but most of those visits are south of the Mason-Dixon line, where they know that there's already support. All these people care about is pushing their ideologies and making sure that their rich friends stay rich and that the power elite remain in control. William Domhoff, author of *Who Rules America?* defines "power elite" as "the leadership group of the upper class. It consists of active-working members of the upper class and high-level employees in profit and non-profit institutions controlled by members of the upper class through stock ownership, financial support, or involvement on the board of directors." http://www2.ucsc.edu/whorulesamerica/power/class_domination.html

PDR is extremely concerned with what comes out of these people's mouths, as their words strike the end of a strong middle class and a power elite continuing to reign supreme. They've never been anything but rich, so why should they care about everyone that's not like them?

In the film *Roger & Me* (1989) by Michael Moore, there's a scene where Moore goes to a country club to speak with a few female members about the many former GM employees who are out of work. The women felt that most of the unemployed workers (you know, the ones who had worked their entire lives for GM and then were just laid off and left with nothing) were just lazy, didn't want to work, and were trying to take the easy way out. They were so far removed from what the real situation was that they couldn't fathom why these people didn't just get another job. Now while these women did express remorse for those losing their jobs and homes, it just goes to show you that while these women lived in the same town as the former-GM workers who were losing everything, they had no understanding of the situation and their first thought was that the former GM employees should just get another job.

This is the problem with the Republican candidates. They cannot sympathize with the middle class because most (if not all) of them have *never been* a part of the middle class. Louis C.K. said it best in his 2005 HBO *One Night Stand Special:* "Poor people know what it's like to be rich, because they fantasize about it constantly … but rich people don't fantasize about being poor, why would they do that?" It's hard to understand the plight of the middle class if you've never been in their shoes or lived their lives. They only know wealth, and in their own words, you'll see how they really do not care about the majority of Americans, but rather their rich circle of cronies.

Mitt Romney

1. Asked if those who criticize the distribution of power and wealth in America were motivated by "jealousy or fairness," Mitt Romney answered, "I think it's about envy. I think it's about class warfare." Romney also cautioned that discussions of inequality should be held "in quiet rooms," ostensibly not in public and televised debate forums.

2. Mitt Romney's infamous declaration that "corporations are people" is a glaring example of the Republican candidate's blindness to the American public. A reported 60 percent of Americans disagree with this statement, and at a time when American faith in government is at a historic low, now should be the time to embrace the public and regain the people's trust, rather than continuing to pander to corporations.

3. Romney, at this point the presumptive GOP Presidential candidate, has based his entire campaign thus far on attacks of President Obama without ever really presenting a positive platform for his own candidacy.

4. Though Mitt Romney continues to try and convince voters that he's just a regular American, recent renovations to his vacation home included an elevator for the GOP candidate's cars.

5. In 2007, a man in a wheelchair suffering from muscular dystrophy met Romney and told him, "I have the support of five of my doctors saying that I am living proof that medical marijuana works," and then asked, "Will you arrest me and my doctors if I get medical marijuana?" Romney interrupted him and moved away saying, "I'm not in favor of medical marijuana being legal." The man in the wheelchair then asked, "So, would you have me arrested?" Romney ignored the man, turned to someone else, and began a conversation as the man in the wheelchair repeated his request for Romney to answer his question.

6. In 2008, Mitt Romney abandoned Americans employed in the auto industry, writing an op-ed entitled, "Let Detroit go bankrupt."

7. Mitt Romney said that America can be "the best place in the world to be middle class again," backing up this claim with examples from The Sports Authority and Staples, companies which Romney's private equity firm Bain Capital had helped to create new jobs. However, a job at these two companies makes under $9 per hour

on average, or $19,090 a year, below the poverty line for a family of three. Meanwhile, Romney made $6,400 an hour at Bain while creating these (low-paying) jobs.

8. Mitt Romney says of his time at Bain Capital, "In those hundreds of businesses we invested in, tens of thousands of jobs net-net were created. I understand how the economy works." However, while it is clear that Bain made huge returns on their investments in companies, exactly where Romney got that "tens of thousands of jobs" figure is murkier; his campaign has not offered statistical evidence of the jobs lost and jobs gained under Romney's direction.

9. Romney argued in a speech to the Ohio Christian Alliance that public education is an "anachronism" left over from the Industrial Revolution "when people came off the farms where they did home school or had a little neighborhood school, and into these big factories ... called public schools."

10. Romney calls the DREAM Act a legislative proposal that helps hardworking youths become American citizens, a "handout." Not only would Romney veto the act, but he also plans to deport all undocumented workers regardless of how long they have resided in America.

11. In February 2012, Mitt Romney held a conference/fundraiser where lobbyists paid $10,000 per person to meet with him and his policy advisers. In essence, Romney is selling influence to representatives from Wall Street, the oil industry, private health insurance companies, and anyone else who can afford the price tag.

12. Romney supporters spent a reported $1,000 per plate and $10,000 per table to have breakfast with the Republican candidate. Protester Richard Blackston, a teacher, was aggravated by how out of touch Romney is with the American people, remarking "I can't even get paper for my classroom."

13. Mitt Romney believes in letting the foreclosure process "run its course and hit the bottom." Romney would do nothing to stop families from losing their homes and would allow the banks to make money off of the hardship of the American middle class.

14. An important part of Romney's platform is his business experience and record of job creation. However, Romney personally profited from buying big companies, shutting down factories, firing workers, and outsourcing jobs overseas.

15. Mitt Romney opposes the elimination of tax incentives and subsidies for major oil companies despite their record-breaking profits in recent months.

16. Romney clings to failed economic policy and creates hardship for working families. His proposed budget would require cuts to programs like Medicare and Social Security that are important to the middle class, while increasing the deficit by trillions of dollars.

17. President Obama's payroll tax cut would give an average of $1,500 back to middle class workers. Mitt Romney called this money being put back in American paychecks a "temporary little Band-Aid."

18. Romney's proposed budget would increase taxes by as much as 60 percent for those making less than $40,000 a year. Middle class families would lose about $167, while those with incomes of over $1 million would receive tax cuts totalling almost $146,000.

19. Romney proposes to hand over control of federal welfare programs to the states and create private sector competition for Medicare services.

20. 49 percent of Romney's proposed tax breaks would go to the top 0.4 percent of households, those making more than $1 million a year.

21. Romney's proposed tax plan increases taxes for people earning less than $10,000 by $112, for those earning $10,000 to $20,000 by $191, for those earning $20,000 to $30,000 by $126, and for those earning $30,000 to $40,000 by $14.

22. Mitt Romney claimed, "Look, I'm not running for the rich people. Rich people can take care of themselves, alright. They're doing just fine. I'm running for middle-class Americans." However, he favors lowering the corporate tax rate, keeping Bush tax cuts for the wealthy, and eliminating the estate tax and has no plan to provide economic relief to working families.

23. Massachusetts fell to 47th out of 50 on job creation while Romney was governor.

24. While Mitt Romney served as Governor of Massachusetts, the wage of the average worker fell by almost 2 percent.

25. Romney publicly opposes birth control and emergency contraception but privately profits from it. His Goldman Sachs 2002 Exchange Place Fund invests in Merck, Mylan, Pfizer, Johnson & Johnson, and Watson Pharmaceuticals, all of which produce birth control. Watson Pharmaceuticals manufactures nine types of emergency contraception.

26. Although Romney calls his wealth "an asset to help America," he has invested millions of dollars in Switzerland and the Cayman Islands. These tax havens for the wealthy cost Americans $100 billion in tax revenue annually.

27. In an attempt to connect with Detroit voters, Romney remarked, "I drive a Mustang and a Chevy pickup truck. Ann drives a couple of Cadillacs, actually." The cars that Romney's wife drives cost $35-50,000 each.

28. Mitt Romney continually proves that he is out of touch with the American public. His frequent references to his own wealth—betting Rick Perry $10,000, remarking that he is not a NASCAR fan but is friends with team owners, reminding voters of the cadillacs he owns—have been called by James Fallows "Romney's gaffe-Tourette's."

29. On June 3 in New Hampshire, Romney was quoted as saying, "I believe the world is getting warmer, and I believe that humans have contributed to that." Less than three months later, also in New Hampshire, he remarked, "Do I think the world's getting hotter? Yeah,

I don't know that but I think that it is. I don't know if it's mostly caused by humans."

30. Romney's campaign is receiving what a consultant calls "supplemental income" from the super PAC Restore Our Future, created solely to support Romney's presidential campaign. Super PAC funding is not subject to contribution limits. "Even though the superPAC may be technically unaffiliated with the candidate's campaign," says Sheila Krumholz of the Center for Responsive Politics, "the donors certainly are tying the two together."

31. In 2011, Romney received campaign contributions at the legal maximum from 172 individuals, 84 percent of the 205 donors to Restore Our Future, a super PAC created to support Romney.

32. Included among these double-donors are five individuals who gave $1 million to Restore Our Future: hedge fund billionaires Julian Robertson, Paul Singer, and John Paulson, homebuilder Bob Perry, and former Bain exec Edward Conrad.

33. Of the total raised for Romney's campaign ($74,053,708) up to February 29, 2012, only 10 percent came from small individuals. Compare that to the figures for Obama's campaign: $157,052,956 raised, and 45 percent from small individuals. This wide gap shows that "small individuals" aren't where Romney's money comes from.

34. Richard Danzig, former Secretary of the Navy on Romney:

"Governor Romney offered his judgment today that Russia is our nation's number one geopolitical foe. This conclusion, as outdated as his ideas on the economy, energy needs, and social issues, is left over from the last century. Does Governor Romney believe that a Cold War foreign policy is the right course in the twenty-first century? Does he believe that Russia is a bigger threat to the U.S. today than terrorism, or cyberwarfare, or a nuclear-armed and erratic North Korea?"

35. Of the companies Bain Capital—the company Romney co-founded and ran—invested in, 22 percent shut down or went bankrupt, resulting in thousands of lost jobs.

36. Romney wrongly asserts: "What unfortunately happens is with all the multiplicity of federal programs, you have massive overhead, with government bureaucrats in Washington administering all these programs, very little of the money that's actually needed by those that really need help, those that can't care for themselves, actually reaches them." He has been proven wrong by the Center on Budget and Policy Priorities, which found that "Medicaid, food stamps (now known as the Supplemental Nutrition Assistance Program, or SNAP), the Supplemental Security Income program for the elderly and disabled poor, housing vouchers, the school lunch and breakfast programs, and the Earned Income Tax Credit show that, in every case, federal administrative costs range from less than 1 percent to 8 percent of total federal program spending."

37. Romney lacks understanding of and experience with foreign policy. He believes that the way to approach going to war with Iran would be to "sit down with your attorneys" and let them "tell you what you have to do."

38. At a Republican presidential debate, Mitt Romney claimed that he would base U.S. policy (that could cost American lives) supporting a regime change in Syria on his belief that Syria is Iran's "route to the sea." However, Iran borders the Arabian and Caspian seas and does not share a border with Syria.

39. Mitt Romney plans to fund the $151 billion in tax cuts to the wealthy with cuts to other programs. His casual attitude towards these programs will hurt many middle class Americans. For instance, contrary to the majority of Americans who support women's rights to their own reproductive care, Romney has said, "Planned Parenthood, we're going to get rid of that."

40. Romney has refused to identify his biggest fundraisers and donors, bringing in millions for his campaign. In other words, the American public has no idea who is buying influence in the GOP.

Seamus the dog and Mitt Romney

41. During a family vacation to Canada in 1983, Romney strapped his dog Seamus to the roof of his car for a twelve-hour drive. This has inspired many animal activists to create a movement called Mitt is Mean,

featuring the tagline: "Will Mitt Romney treat you like a dog if he's President? Let's hope not."

42. David Kravitz of Blue Mass Group called it "classic Romney: it solves a problem efficiently, in a business-like manner, and with no regard whatsoever for the suffering that the solution may cause."

43. Gail Collins: "Elect Mitt Romney and he will take the nation on the road to the future. Some of us will be stuck on the roof."

44. Romney told Chris Wallace at Fox News that it was a "completely airtight kennel" that Seamus was "comfortable" in, saying that the dog "climbed up there regularly, enjoyed himself. He was in a kennel at home a great deal of the time as well. We loved the dog."

Michele Bachmann

45. Michele Bachmann's beliefs are foreign to most Americans and even most Christians. She belongs to a particularly conservative subset of the Christian right with beliefs more extreme than those of any politician like her, including Sarah Palin.

46. "When you talk about extending the current reduced tax rate on the people who are job providers, that only makes sense in a down economy. We want to create jobs. That helps to create jobs, to keep more money in the pockets of the job creator. When you pull more money out of the pockets of the job creators, you're going to have less jobs. What do we need in the United

States right now? More jobs, millions of jobs, high-paying jobs. President Obama hasn't delivered. The only way to do that, Chris, is make sure businesses have all of the money they need to be able to create jobs. Right now, they don't."

47. Bachmann claims that corporations are not hiring because they lack the money. However, according to the *Wall Street Journal*, corporations have more money now than they have in nearly fifty years. Business are filling their own coffers rather than hiring or investing in new plants. Nonfinancial corporations held over $2 trillion in liquid assets last June, up from $88 billion last March. 7.1 percent of all company assets was cash, the highest percentage since 1963.

48. Michele Bachmann: "Our nation needs to stop doing for people what they can and should do for themselves. Self reliance means, if anyone will not work, neither should he eat."

49. Bachmann seems to advocate slave wages, stating, "If we took away the minimum wage—if conceivably it was gone—we could potentially virtually wipe out unemployment completely."

Rick Santorum

50. "'You're not going to find the perfect candidate unless it's Jesus Christ," Jim Duggar [television's famous father of nineteen children] said on Monday. With the Christian messiah sitting this one out, Duggar endorsed his second choice: Rick Santorum.

51. Santorum has said that he would vote against extending President Obama's payroll tax cut, which gives middle-class individuals an average of $1,500 back in their paychecks.

52. Of Red, White & Blue PAC's fourteen individual donors, nine contributed the maximum amount to campaign committee of Rick Santorum, the super PAC's favored candidate.

53. Rick Santorum: "We are seeing it. We are seeing the fabric of this country fall apart, and it's falling apart because of single moms."

54. Rick Santorum: "What we have is moms raising children in single-parent households simply breeding more criminals."

55. Santorum staff member Jamie Johnson reportedly circulated a sexist email, urging Christian voters not to support a female candidate. Johnson allegedly wrote, "The question then comes, 'Is it God's highest desire, that is, his biblically expressed will, … to have a woman rule the institutions of the family, the church, and the state?'"

56. In the following Rick Santorum campaign speech excerpt, he claims he was misinterpreted and did not say "black" but "blah": "I don't want to make black people's lives better by giving them somebody else's money. I want to give them the opportunity to go out and earn the money and provide for themselves and their families." Santorum later defended himself by saying, "In fact, I'm pretty confident I didn't say black.

What I think—I started to say a word and then sort of changed and it sort of—blah—mumbled it and sort of changed my thought."

57. Tea Party Rep. Paul Ryan's proposed budget plan would effectively end Medicare and force seniors to pay double for their health care. Santorum thinks that Ryan's drastic cuts to federal programs aren't extreme enough, saying "I support in principle what Paul Ryan is suggesting. The only concern I have is I don't think Paul Ryan goes far enough."

58. Rick Santorum, suggesting that he would support outlawing pre- or extra-marital sex: "One of the things I will talk about, that no president has talked about before, is I think the dangers of contraception in this country. It's not okay. It's a license to do things in a sexual realm that is counter to how things are supposed to be. [Sex] is supposed to be within marriage. It's supposed to be for purposes that are yes, conjugal…but also procreative."

Ron Paul

59. Ron Paul has been criticized for controversial newsletters written under his name in the 80s and 90s that included paranoid conspiracy theories, bigotry, and racism. Paul has denied writing the newsletters and rejects their content, claiming that this has always been his stance. Paul said on CNN, "I never read that stuff. I never—I would never—I came—I was probably aware of it 10 years after it was written… Well, you know, we talked about [the newsletters] twice yesterday at CNN. Why don't you

go back and look at what I said yesterday on CNN, and what I've said for 20-some years. It was 22 years ago. I didn't write them. I disavow them and that's it."

However, in 1996 Paul did not deny authorship and defended some of the more egregiously racist claims in the newsletters, objecting only that his words were taken out of context.

60. In 1999, Ron Paul was the only member of Congress to oppose the issuing of a Congressional Gold Medal to Rosa Parks.

61. In May 2011, Ron Paul said in an interview that he opposes the Civil Rights Act of 1964.

Rick Perry

62. Rick Perry's campaign has been receiving double-funding from some of his wealthiest supporters. Perry has received donations from eleven individuals giving the legal maximum who are also contributors to the super PAC Americans for Rick Perry. An even larger super PAC, Make Us Great Again, backing Perry is also primarily funded by people who have maxed out to Perry.

63. $12.3 million of Rick Perry's fundraising came from donors giving the maximum $2,500 contribution allowed by law. Approximately 4 percent of his campaign money was from small donors, giving under $200 at a time. This percentage of small donations is very low compared to his competitors.

64. Of the total raised for Perry's campaign ($19,889,190) up to February 29, 2012, only 5 percent came from small individuals. Compare that to the figures for Obama's campaign: $157,052,956 raised, and 45 percent from small individuals. This wide gap shows the "small individuals" aren't where Perry's money comes from.

Newt Gingrich

65. Winning Our Future, the biggest super PAC backing GOP candidate Newt Gingrich, receives a significant portion of its funding from individuals who have already donated the legal maximum to Gingrich's campaign—both for the general election and the primaries. This does not take into consideration the reported $10 million given to the super PAC in support of Gingrich by casino titan Sheldon Adelson and his wife, who also donated the legal maximum to Gingrich's primary campaign.

General Commentary/Information:

66. Jon Huntsman on the Republican candidates for 2012: "We have people on the Republican side too far to the right. We have zero substance. We have no good ideas that are being circulated or talking about that allow the country to get back on its feet economically so we begin creating jobs."

67. At the 2012 GOP presidential debate in Iowa, the words "middle class" were never uttered.

68. Michele Bachmann, Herman Cain, Rick Perry, and Rick Santorum have all publicly stated that God asked them to run for office.

69. All of the 2012 GOP candidates call for trillions of dollars in tax cuts for the individuals and corporations who are already wealthiest. At the same time, they want to end Medicare as we know it and cut funding to federal programs like Social Security and Medicaid that many Americans rely on.

Elite Media Personalities

70. Ann Coulter: "I think [women] should be armed but should not vote ... women have no capacity to understand how money is earned. They have a lot of ideas on how to spend it ... it's always more money on education, more money on child care, more money on day care."

71. Ann Coulter: "It would be a much better country if women did not vote. That is simply a fact. In fact, in every presidential election since 1950—except Goldwater in '64—the Republican would have won, if only the men had voted."

72. Ann Coulter: "You would think there were 'Straights Only' water fountains the way Democrats carry on so (as if any gay man would drink nonbottled water)."

73. Ann Coulter: "Frankly, I'm not a big fan of the First Amendment."

74. Rush Limbaugh: "You know, this is all BS, as far as I'm concerned. Cross species evolution, I don't think anybody's ever proven that. They're going out of their way now to establish evolution as a mechanism for creation, which, of course, you can't do."

75. Rush Limbaugh referred to female Cabinet members as "Sex-retaries"

76. Limbaugh also likes referring to anyone who questions gender inequality a "feminazi."

77. Jane Fonda, Robin Morgan, and Gloria Steinem have called for the FCC to take Rush Limbaugh off the air for his "regular doses of hate speech."

78. On his radio program *Savage Nation*, Michael Savage was discussing the inhumane abuse that went on in Abu Ghraib (which he called "Grab-an-Arab prison"): "I don't mean to be too comedic in the political arena, but these so called abuse photos frankly are mild by comparisons to what goes on in South of Market clubs in San Francisco."

79. Glenn Beck, while discussing the DREAM Act's plan to make it legal for children of immigrants to go to college or join the military, used his radio show as a platform to spread misinformation that the legislation would create preferential circumstances for children of immigrants over American citizens. He even introduced racial undertones, saying, "if you're white or you're an American citizen or a white American citizen, you're pretty much toast."

Fox News:

80. Fox News blames the Obama administration for the rising price of gasoline, although this claim has been rejected by energy analysts. In 2008, when the average price of gasoline hit a record $4.11, Fox said that "no President has the power to increase or to lower gas prices."

81. Sean Hannity: "It doesn't say anywhere in the Constitution this idea of the separation of church and state."

CHAPTER TWO

SCIENCE AND HEALTH

And then, there are fossils. Whenever anybody tries to tell me that it [the creation of Earth] took place in seven days, I reach for a fossil, and go "fossil." And if they keep talking, I throw it just over their head.
— Lewis Black, *Red, White and Screwed* (2006)

When it comes to science, the majority of the Republican Party believes in creationism over evolution. Now normally, we at PDR would have no problem with this. If someone feels strongly about their personal religious beliefs, then all the power to them. Religion has helped many people across the globe in times of struggle, loss, and need. It has been around since the dawn of man, and while some people are stronger believers than others, there's no reason that both groups cannot coexist. Our founding fathers felt that there should be a separation from church and state, and we happen to agree. The problem we're seeing in America today (and especially with the Republican Party), is that not only do they feel that there should be no separation, but they are now using what they've learned in their religion to make government decisions. Some people may have felt that in Al Gore's film, *An Inconvenient*

Truth (2006), the information he gathered was from scientific research. In the case of global warming, most Republicans take the side of their faith to "debunk" this, and use religion as a means to counter what scientists have found through extensive research. Now, there are facts, and then there are beliefs. Facts have evidence, while beliefs are more personal. We've all watched people argue about this, and even though one person may have all the facts to prove that they are right, the one who has the personal beliefs will never back down. Unfortunately, for the sake of this country, the people with the personal beliefs aren't just everyday people. They are, in fact, running for an office that will have the ultimate power over the entire country. To them, faith is sounder than science, and until scientists can prove creationism, most Republicans will always side against them.

When it comes to health, and specifically, health care, it goes back to what we said in the previous chapter. Around the time that this book was written, the seventy-one-year-old former Vice-President Dick Cheney received a heart transplant. There is no doubt that he has incredible medical coverage, and while the usual cut-off age for a heart transplant is sixty, he was still able to have it done. Unfortunately for most people in this country, they cannot even afford to go to the doctor for a check-up. There have been numerous stories in the news over the past few years of people who could not afford the proper medication for an illness, and ended up losing their lives because of it.

Universal healthcare is successful in many countries. While there will always be those that feel there are too many problems with it, the thought that there are people out there who are against their fellow countrymen and women having health coverage is absolutely criminal. Everyone should be able to go to the doctor or the hospital when they are sick, and just because the power elite have never had to worry about not having coverage, doesn't give them the right to tell others that they do not deserve. Not everyone is as lucky as them to be financially "well-off," and having the mindset that those less-fortunate don't deserve it is an absurd way of thinking. Sadly, as you'll see below, there are many people in power that think this exact way.

Science and Evolution

82. Michelle Bachmann believes that evolution is just a theory that has "never been proven," and that schools should teach intelligent design.

83. Senator Tom Coburn (R-OK) said that "Global warming is just a lot of crap."

84. Bill Haslam, the Republican Governor of Tennessee has announced that he is likely to sign a bill that attacks schools for teaching evolution to students. This piece of legislation echoes the Scopes Monkey Trial of the 1920s, demonstrating yet again that the Republicans and their policy are stuck far in the past.

85. Conservapedia, the conservative answer to Wikipedia, contains a nearly 6,000-word entry refuting the theory of relativity. "Relativity has been met with much resistance in the scientific world," says the site. It claims that liberals have "extrapolated the theory" to advance their agendas. "Virtually no one who is taught and believes Relativity continues to read the Bible," Conservapedia goes on, "a book that outsells New York Times bestsellers by a hundred-fold."

The site then goes on to provide "counterexamples" to relativity, including "evidence" from the Bible.

86. Conservapedia claims somewhat strangely that relativity has not led to the creation of any important or useful technology. In reality, GPS devices, PET scans, and particle accelerators all rely on a fundamental understanding of relativity.

87. Conservapedia does not seem concerned with the existence of concrete evidence or scientific fact. Conservative activist Phyllis Schlafly has said of the site that it "strengthened my faith. I don't have to live with what's printed in the newspaper. I don't have to take what's put out by Wikipedia. We've got our own way to express knowledge, and the more that we can clear out the liberal bias that erodes our faith, the better."

88. As the 2012 election campaigns began to take shape, Republican Jon Huntsmann broke with his party's tendency to reject scientific fact, tweeting: "To be clear, I believe in evolution and trust scientists on global warming. Call me crazy."

89. The findings of a study published in the American Sociological Review show that while overall trust in science has generally been stable since 1974, among self-identified conservatives, trust in science is at an all-time low.

90. "Conservatives with high school degrees, bachelor's degrees, and graduate degrees all experienced greater distrust in science over time and these declines are statistically significant. In addition, a comparison of predicted

probabilities indicates that conservatives with college degrees decline more quickly than those with only a high school degree. These results are quite profound, because they imply that conservative discontent with science was not attributable to the uneducated but to rising distrust among educated conservatives."

91. Only 18 percent of Republicans and Tea Party members accept the scientifically proven idea that global warming is caused by humans, and 45 percent of Republicans and 43 percent respectively believe in human evolution. The beliefs of political conservatives are in conflict with modern knowledge and scientific fact.

92. "Climate science has basically been at the receiving end of the best-funded, best-organized smear campaign by the wealthiest industry that the Earth has ever known—that's the bottom line," says Michael Mann, a climatologist known for creating the "hockey stick" graph, which indicates that the dramatic temperature increase in the past 100 years is because of humans.

93. Rep. John Shimkus, potentially the future chairman of the committee in Congress dealing with energy and the environment believes that climate change is no cause for concern because "God said he wouldn't destroy the Earth after Noah's flood."

94. John Shimkus: "Now, do I believe in climate change? In my trip to Greenland, the answer is yes. The climate is changing. The question is more about the costs and benefits and trying to spend taxpayer dollars on something that you cannot stop versus the changes that have been occurring forever. That's the real debate."

95. John Shimkus: "It's plant food … So if we decrease the use of carbon dioxide, are we not taking away plant food from the atmosphere? … So all our good intentions could be for naught. In fact, we could be doing just the opposite of what the people who want to save the world are saying."

    The National Wildlife Fund debunked this theory, noting that plants were around long before humans figured out how to burn fossil fuels.

96. The quote John Shimkus used to dismiss spending government money on the climate crisis was Matthew 24:31: "The Earth will end only when God declares it's time to be over. Man will not destroy this Earth. This Earth will not be destroyed by a Flood," Shimkus asserted. "I do believe that God's word is infallible, unchanging, perfect."

97. Although there is a scientific consensus that carbon dioxide and other heat-trapping emissions are to blame for global warming, ExxonMobil has spent $16 million manufacturing uncertainty about climate change. Many of these organizations funded by ExxonMobil all share the same staff serving as spokespeople and scientific consultants.

98. Newt Gingrich refers to the EPA's fracking regulations and President Obama's desire to end tax breaks for oil companies as an "assault on American energy."

99. Rick Santorum's home state of Pennsylvania is one of the main sites of both fracking and criticisms of its negative environmental impact. Santorum outright dismisses this

environmental concern, saying, "It's a new way to try and scare you. Let me tell you what is going to happen—nothing is going to happen."

100. Mitt Romney criticizes the EPA's attempt to regulate fracking, characterizing it as a power play to "move the whole economy away from oil, gas, coal, nuclear and push it into the renewables."

101. Rick Santorum called climate change "a hoax" and championed an energy plan that relies heavily on fossil fuels.

102. Rick Santorum: "We were put on this Earth as creatures of God to have dominion over the Earth, to use it wisely and steward it wisely, but for our benefit not for the Earth's benefit."

103. Santorum called climate change "an absolute travesty of scientific research that was motivated by those who, in my opinion, saw this as an opportunity to create a panic and a crisis for government to be able to step in and even more greatly control your life."

104. Rick Santorum: "I for one never bought the hoax. I for one understand just from science that there are one hundred factors that influence the climate. To suggest that one minor factor of which man's contribution is a minor factor in the minor factor is the determining ingredient in the sauce that affects the entire global warming and cooling is just absurd on its face. And yet we have politicians running to the ramparts—unfortunately politicians who happen to be running for the Republican nomination for president—who

bought into man-made global warming and bought into cap and trade."

105. Rick Santorum: "I believe we don't know [if there is climate change as a result of humans]. I am an amateur paleontologist. The planet has changed its temperature a number of times … If you look at the Antarctic today, you'll figure it [must've been] a lot warmer when the dinosaurs were there. So what I've said in the past is I'm happy to take prudent measures that aren't very expensive."

106. Rick Santorum: "We have the Endangered Species Act, which has prevented us from timbering all sorts of acreage there. It's bankrupted the school district and the like because of the government's inability to allow for us to care for our resources. A forest in my opinion is like a garden and you've got to care for it. If you don't care for it, you leave it to nature and nature will do what it does: boom and bust."

107. Austin Scott (R-GA) accused the EPA of using "Gestapo tactics" for its decision to fine a landlord who used lead-based paint on his properties without his tenants' consent.

108. Former House Majority Leader Tom DeLay once referred to the EPA as "the Gestapo of Government."

109. GOP Senator Jim Inhofe called the EPA a "Gestapo bureaucracy."

110. 236 Republicans in Congress voted in favor of legislation that would prevent any effort on the part of the EPA "to

implement, administer, or enforce any statutory or regulatory requirement pertaining to emissions of greenhouse gases." In other words, Republicans are trying to hinder all of the EPA's measures to protect the environment.

111. Republicans efforts undermining the EPA are unpopular with the public. Two thirds of Americans are against Newt Gingrich's plan to abolish the EPA, 63 percent of the country thinks the government should do more to hold polluters accountable, and almost 70 percent think that EPA scientists, not Congress, should set pollution standards.

112. On climate change, Rick Perry, former governor of Texas falsely claims: "We are seeing almost weekly, or even daily, scientists are coming forward and questioning the original idea that man-made global warming is what is causing the climate to change."

113. Former Utah governor and contender for the Republican presidential nomination, Jon Huntsman, Jr., says the Republican Party is becoming the "anti-science party."

114. On evolution, Ron Paul has said, "I think it's a theory and I don't accept it as a theory."

115. Rick Perry denies scientific evidence and claims, "I'm not sure anybody actually knows completely and absolutely how old the earth is."

116. Michele Bachmann has embraced the idea that the HPV vaccine can cause mental retardation, despite there being no proof to backup the claim, simply because a woman came up to her and told her so.

117. Herman Cain's 9-9-9 tax proposal requires its own sort of economics, inconsistent with truth and mathematic principle.

118. Republican "climate skeptics" have attacked meteorologist Paul Douglas for acknowledging climate change based on peer-reviewed studies and empirical data, despite being a Republican himself. He's been forced to defend his stance claiming "acknowledging climate science doesn't make you a liberal" and has even urged Republicans to separate identity politics from science—apparently to little avail.

119. "Completely wrong." "Simply ignorant." "Scientifically incorrect." "Utter Nonsense." "Very odd." These are words scientists have used in the past to describe the nationally televised ramblings of weather forecaster Joe Bastardi, who Fox News hosts from time to time in an apparent effort to dismantle whatever its viewers might know about physics.

120. Bastardi: "CO2 cannot cause global warming. I'll tell you why. It doesn't mix well with the atmosphere, for one. For two, its specific gravity is one and a half times that of the rest of the atmosphere. It heats and cools much quicker. Its radiative processes are much different. So it cannot—it literally cannot cause global warming."

    Asked about Bastardi's statements, Kerry Emanuel of MIT said: "Utter rubbish. Sorry to be so direct, but that is just the case." NASA climatologist Gavin Schmidt added: "Bastardi is attempting to throw out 150 years of physics." "He seems very confused," said physicist Richard Muller."

121. Fox's Tracy Byrnes: "The Temperature Basically Hasn't Changed Much Since The Ice Age."

122. In a tremendous demonstration of misinformation, Michele Bachmann stated that "Carbon dioxide is not a harmful gas; it is a harmless gas … And yet we're being told that we have to reduce this natural substance and reduce the American standard of living to create an arbitrary reduction in something that is naturally occurring in the Earth."

123. Herman Cain: "I don't believe … global warming is real. Do we have climate change? Yes. Is it a crisis? No. … Because the science, the real science, doesn't say that we have any major crisis or threat when it comes to climate change."

124. Rick Santorum: "I'm not comfortable with intelligent design being taught in the science classroom. What we should be teaching are the problems and holes, and I think there are legitimate problems and holes in the theory of evolution. And what we need to do is to present those fairly from a scientific point of view … And we should lay out areas in which the evidence supports evolution and the areas in the evidence that does not."

125. Rick Santorum: "I believe in Genesis 1:1—God created the heavens and the earth."

126. Bill Nye "The Science Guy" appeared on the Fox Business Network to discuss climate change, but was told by host Charles Payne that his scientific evidence was "confusing our viewers."

127. James E. Hansen, a climatologist at NASA who heads NASA's Goddard Institute for Space Studies in New York, spoke out against the restraints on climate change information placed by the Bush Administration: "In my more than three decades in government, I have never seen anything approaching the degree to which information flow from scientists to the public has been screened and controlled as it has now." He also said that contrary to the administration's wishes to wait ten years to evaluate climate change, "delay of another decade… is a colossal risk."

128. Bush-appointed George C. Deutsch resigned from his position as a writer and editor of NASA's public affairs because he lied on his résumé. Deutsch limited press access to NASA climatologist James Hansen to decrease spotlight on the issue of global warming, and he also told a NASA web designer to add the word "theory" after any mention of the Big Bang.

129. Conservapedia 's entry for "dinosaurs" states that dinosaurs came into being on day 6 of creation roughly 6,000 years ago. Meanwhile, carbon dating of fossils proves that dinosaurs have been extinct for 65 million years.

Health Care

130. Rep. Michele Bachmann (R-MN) claims health care is "an opportunity that some people choose to engage in, but 40 million people do not. And the premise was made that people don't buy insurance because they can't afford it. That's not true. These are people who

just decide they want to roll the dice and take their chances that they won't need insurance."

131. Michele Bachmann supported a proposal from the Republican Study Committee to cut Medicare benefits more dramatically than outlined in Paul Ryan's plan, get rid of 1 million jobs, and radically decrease funding for low-income families, schools, and law enforcement.

132. Newt Gingrich has said that Republicans want to do away with Medicare, but prefer to let it "wither on the vine" for political reasons. In 1995, Gingrich compared Medicare to Russian bureaucracy.

133. Republicans in Congress support the Blunt-Rubio Amendment, which would allow employers and insurance companies to choose which health benefits to provide based on their own moral beliefs, rather than allowing employees (and their doctors) to determine the health care that they require.

134. The Republican-controlled House voted to cut all $75 million in federal funding to Planned Parenthood and the $317 million Title X budget. This money would have helped a reported 4.7 million Americans gain access to health care services such as cancer screening, STD testing, prenatal care, sex education, and birth control.

135. Republicans want to end Medicare's guarantee of health insurance for seniors and slash Social Security benefits. These kinds of cuts would necessitate tremendous reductions in the services that many families rely on.

136. Republicans oppose the Affordable Care Act, which would give 31 million previously uninsured Americans access to health care.

137. Rick Perry claims in his book, *Fed Up! Our Fight to Save America from Washington*, that the government controls how much salt Americans can have: "We are fed up with being overtaxed and overregulated. We are tired of being told how much salt we can put on our food, what windows we can buy for our house, what kind of cars we can drive, what kinds of guns we can own, what kind of prayers we are allowed to say and where we can say them, what political speech we are allowed to use to elect candidates, what kind of energy we can use, what kind of food we can grow, what doctor we can see and countless other restrictions on our right to live as we see fit."

138. The conservative Supreme Court undercut President Obama's health care law, questioning the constitutionality of requiring states to expand Medicaid to cover more Americans in poverty. However, under the Affordable Care Act, the federal government covers over 90 percent of the cost of extending coverage to more impoverished Americans, and each state is only responsible for carrying out its own program, as has been the case since 1965 when Medicaid was established.

139. This year, Republicans have waged an attack on women's health by going after Planned Parenthood, attempting to do away with the legal concept of Statutory Rape, trying to overturn the Affordable Care Act, and working against Title X, the only government grant devoted to family planning.

140. Mitt Romney told reporters, "Planned Parenthood, we're going to get rid of that." Romney believes that Planned Parenthood—an organization that has provided health care to 20 percent of American women—is too expensive, while tax cuts for corporations and the wealthiest Americans seem to fit into his budget just fine.

141. Paul Ryan's budget would turn Medicare into a voucher program. Rather than giving seniors the coverage that they have paid for throughout their working lives, Rep. Ryan would have them pay out of pocket for their health care.

142. Rep. Paul Ryan's budget would cut over $1 trillion from Medicaid, thereby depriving up to 60 million Americans of coverage, including pregnant women, nursing home patients, and low-income children.

143. Under Ryan's plan, Medicaid enrollment would be 44 million people fewer than what projections under the current law predict.

144. Women currently pay up to 50 percent more than men for the same insurance coverage. The Affordable Care Act eliminates gender rating, meaning that being a woman will no longer be a pre-existing condition. If Romney or Santorum is elected, gender inequality in health care will continue.

145. In 2010, the Republican battlecry was "repeal and replace" with respect to Obamacare. However, if the Supreme Court does find the law to be unconstitutional, Republicans have offered no plan to replace

the Affordable Care Act. This would leave the roughly 50 million uninsured Americans out in the cold.

146. Florida Governor Rick Scott has cut workers' benefits, rejected much of the federal government's money for health care, and kept Medicaid recipients on edge about the cost of their care. However, he pays only $30 each month for his own health insurance. Scott and his dependents reportedly pay 20 percent of what a janitor in Florida's Capitol pays for his health insurance, and a mere 3 percent of what a retired state trooper pays for his coverage. Questioned about these glaring inconsistencies, Scott said these were "private matters."

147. Tea Party Rep. Joe Walsh of Illinois talks about how irresponsible it is to leave the national debt to our children and grandchildren. Walsh owes over $115,000 in overdue child support payments.

148. In addition to the fact that Americans are entitled to Medicare and Social Security because we pay for them, both programs have been self-sustaining while successfully meeting the needs of the millions who rely on them.

149. Medicare costs much less than private health care. If the richest 10 percent—those with incomes over $106,800—paid their full share, Social Security would not be in grave danger of shortfall.

150. Although Republicans like to call programs like Social Security and Medicare "handouts," a report by the Center on Budget and Policy Priorities indicates that over 90 percent of entitlements go to the elderly or disabled, or working Americans in need of additional assistance. A mere 9 percent of entitlement money goes to employable

Americans who are not working, and most of those dollars go to medical costs, unemployment, and survivor benefits.

151. Many conservatives see Obamacare as a governmental takeover of health care, creating, as Sarah Palin called them, "death panels" to make end-of-life care decisions for the ill and elderly. Many republicans also believe that Obamacare will increase the deficit, cut benefits to Medicare recipients, fund abortions, and pay for the health care of illegal immigrants. All of these claims are false.

152. The Republican party's current unwillingness to compromise is astounding. Their all-or-nothing strategies prevented them from reaching satisfactory agreements on health care and government spending. A party that was more moderate and more willing to negotiate would certainly have seen more results in their favor. Current Republicans seem determined to stick to their inflexible strategy, however ill-advised and impractical, as evidenced by their enthusiastic espousal of Paul Ryan's budget, which was notably unpopular with voters.

153. By opposing health care reform ending the practice of denying insurance coverage to people with pre-existing conditions, GOP Rep. Austin Scott would prevent hundreds of thousands of citizens from having the necessary health care coverage.

154. Senator Jim Inhofe stated that he will vote without reading the 1,000-page health care reform bill: "I don't have to read it, or know what's in it. I'm going to oppose it anyways."

155. Every GOP Presidential candidate pledges to repeal "Obamacare," forcibly depriving people of health care coverage by reinstating pre-existing conditions as an obstacle to gaining coverage on the private market. Repealing Obama's plan would also strip 2.5 million young adults of their coverage, as they would no longer be eligible to receive benefits from their parents' health plans.

156. In April 2011, 40 Senate and 235 House Republicans voted for Rep. Paul Ryan's plan to convert Medicare to a voucher system that would make millions of senior citizens victims of the private insurance marketplace.

157. GOP Congressman Denny Rehberg said that expanding Medicaid and giving subsidies to low and middle-class Americans is like springing for the "expensive vacation home" that the average person would not buy while facing a deficit as staggering as America's.

158. In 2009, the wife of a brain-injury victim whose health insurance will not cover the cost of his food asked Senator Tom Coburn (R-OK) where she could turn for help. The Senator responded that "the idea that the government is a solution to our problems is an inaccurate, a very inaccurate statement."

159. In their attacks on the Affordable Care Act, Republicans often criticize what they call "welfare" and "handouts," and remind Americans that they must earn the coverage they are given. However, Congress Republicans have no concrete plans to create jobs and direct more and more resources to corporations and the 1 percent. In other words, they are content to keep millions of Americans deprived of health care.

160. Democrats in congress proposed legislation providing health care benefits for 9/11 first responders at Ground Zero, but Republicans subsequently killed this bill.

161. Jonathan Gruber was the health consultant who "helped Governor Romney develop his health care reform, or 'Romneycare,' before going down to Washington to help President Obama develop his national version of that law [Obamacare]." But while Romney at first set out to make Massachusetts a model of health care for the nation, Jonathan Gruber noted that "all of a sudden, Mitt Romney started attacking what he'd done." While campaigning, Mitt Romney has said, "I will repeal Obamacare and I'll kill it dead on its first day."

162. Madelyn Rhenisch, the first enrollee in Core Health Plan under Romneycare, feels that Romney is "jumping to a political position where the issue isn't health care, it's getting elected." She was invited to Romneycare's initiation ceremony, where Romney heard her story and many others of people who reclaimed their lives thanks to the healthcare reforms he's recently turned his back on. However, now she asks of Romney's change of heart, "Don't we matter?"

Sexuality and Reproductive Health

163. Many conservatives—especially on the Christian Right— claim that having an abortion increases a woman's risk of breast cancer or mental disorders. There is no scientific evidence backing up this claim.

164. The Christian Right claim that fetuses can perceive pain at twenty weeks of gestation, although a study in 2005 by the University of California–San Francisco, found that "fetal perception of pain is unlikely before

the third trimester," or about twenty-seven weeks into the pregnancy.

Conservatives also feel that:

165. Same-sex parenting is bad for kids.

166. Homosexuality is a disorder, or a choice, and is curable through therapy.

167. Republican Rep. Jeanine Notter of New Hampshire has claimed birth control pills cause prostate cancer without the backing of science.

168. The New Hampshire House of representatives has passed a bill requiring doctors to tell women seeking abortions that the procedure can cause breast cancer, despite there being no proven scientific link.

169. Representative Alan Dick (R-AK) is in favor of legislation requiring a woman to have written paternal permission in order to terminate a pregnancy. Ostensibly, this law would apply even in cases of rape and incest.

170. In 2012, Republicans have introduced nearly 430 restrictions limiting access to abortions.

171. It is no secret that Republicans favor abstinence-only sex education, in spite of research proving time and again that this method is ineffective. According to studies at the University of Washington, states with abstinence-only policies on average had higher rates of teen pregnancy than states requiring comprehensive sex education.

172. Kansas House Republicans have passed what they refer to as the "Abortion Conscience" Bill. This bill would allow doctors and medical facilities to refuse access to birth control or any drug that might lead to abortion if their personal moral beliefs are against a woman's right to choose. It also allows medical professionals to refuse to help patients find other providers of the care that they will not provide. This bill allows Republicans to project their personal views onto women's bodies and could bar victims of sexual assault from getting the time-sensitive medical care they need to prevent pregnancy.

173. Republican Senator Olympia Snowe has criticized her own party's fixation with limiting a woman's access to contraception, calling it "a retro-debate that took place in the 1950s," and further saying that it was "surprising in the 21st century we would be revisiting this issue."

174. When Lester Crawford was acting director of the FDA and was on his way to moving up to permanent director by President Bush, Hillary Clinton and Patty Murray (D-WA) wanted to block the nomination because Crawford's refusal to allow Plan B to be available over the counter was based on ideology, not science (and the advice of an FDA expert panel).

CHAPTER THREE

HISTORIC REPUBLICAN HIJINKS

Throughout our history, Republicans have been known for saying and doing some pretty stupid things. We'd make a list, but then the title of this book would be *1,001 Ways That the Republican Party Has Shown Their Incompetence*. But as you know, that is not the case. Whether it's Dan Quayle telling a twelve-year-old that potato has an "e" at the end, or George W. Bush not knowing his left hand from his right, Republicans have consistently screwed-up in the public eye. The sad part is, while these can be looked at as "bloopers," many of their slip-ups have been a bit more devastating.

While it's fun to laugh when Republicans misspeak or trip in public, it stops being funny they decide not to react for days when there's a natural disaster (Hurricane Katrina) or make decisions that affect millions of people purely to spite another person. The best of the best should be running our country. These are people who are supposed to be looking out for us, making the best possible decisions to improve our way of life. The only problem is, as we've seen with most Republican presidents and candidates, that they do what's best for their own interests, and that is when we see decisions made that end up biting us in the behind.

WMD anyone?

175. In 1990, the campaign of Senator Jesse Helms (R-NC) was shown to be guilty of voter caging when his campaign targeted homes in predominantly black areas by mailing out pamphlets challenging their residency and the legitimacy of their voter registration.

176. Republican President Warren G. Harding's administration was among the most corrupt in history. Harding peopled his cabinet with his friends, who came to be known as the "Ohio Gang." Many of these men were charged with bribery and corruption and later resigned, while a few committed suicide rather than stand trial.

177. Most notable perhaps was when President Harding's Secretary of the Interior, Albert Fall, sold the rights to federal oil reserves located in Teapot Dome, Wyoming, in exchange for personal loans and cattle. He was eventually convicted and sent to prison.

178. Ulysses S. Grant's presidency is infamous for the "Whiskey Ring" scandal, which involved Republican government agents and politicians conspiring with whiskey distillers and distributors to divert tax revenue for their own personal gain.

179. In 2001, GOP chairman Charles Cagle pled guilty to conspiracy to commit bank fraud and conspiracy to commit money laundering.

180. Lawrence E. King, Jr., a major GOP fundraiser, was convicted of conspiracy, embezzlement, and keeping false records for a credit union in Omaha, Nebraska.

181. In the mid-1990s, conservatives attempted to destroy America's social safety net. Newt Gingrich attempted to do away with unemployment insurance and financial aid for those in poverty, while at the same time ensuring that his district in Georgia received more in "federal subsidies than any suburban county in the country, with two exceptions: Arlington Virginia, effectively part of the Federal Government, and Brevard County Florida, the home of the Kennedy Space Center."

182. In 2006, President Bush unexpectedly fired eleven Republican federal prosecutors whom he had appointed. When questioned about this arbitrary decision, Bush and his advisors simply claimed executive privilege.

183. In 1996, Republican Governor Pete Wilson signed energy deregulation legislation for the state of California, leading to a rise in utility pricing, and eventually to California's 2000–2001 electricity supply crisis and statewide blackouts.

184. In 2001, President Bush allowed the federal mandate for wholesale generators to sell power to the state of California to expire and testified in opposition to bringing back price caps and attempting to re-regulate the utilities, allowing the blackouts to worsen.

185. In 1864, the construction company Crédit Mobilier was founded to build the Union Pacific Railroad. The promoters, including Oakes Ames, a Congressman from Massachusetts, were later charged with profiteering.

This incident represents the Republican party's lax business ethics during American Reconstruction.

186. With Democratic President Jimmy Carter in office, the national debt hit a historic low of $980 billion in 1980. Over the next twelve years, Presidents Reagan and Bush allowed the national debt to soar to $3.2 trillion.

187. Prohibition was technically enacted in 1919 at the end of the presidency of Woodrow Wilson, whose veto was overridden by a Republican Congress. However, the 18th amendment to the Constitution and the Volstead Act were created by Republicans, written by Republicans, and supported by Republicans Harding, Coolidge, and Hoover.

188. Republican Senator Joe McCarthy callously wielded accusations of Communism and Communist sympathizing like an axe at the heads of many Americans, both citizen and politician, from 1950 until the Senate found it necessary to censure him in 1954.

189. Republican President Herbert Hoover has been crowned by *U.S. News & World Report* as one of the ten worst American Presidents for his role in exacerbating the Great Depression.

190. In fact, almost half of the ten worst Presidents in American history, according to *U.S. News & World Report*, are members of the Republican Party, with most of the remainder consisting largely of members of the defunct Whig party.

191. In November 1995, major portions of the federal government suspended operations when a Republican-controlled Congress refused to raise the debt ceiling after unsuccessfully attempting to enact cuts on Medicare. Rumor has it that then Speaker of the House Newt Gingrich had been snubbed by President Clinton on a flight months earlier, and this petty personal matter may have partly caused the shutdown.

192. The Watergate Scandal of the 1970s was the result of a politically-motivated break-in at the Democratic National Committee headquarters in Washington D.C., and the following attempt to cover it up by Republican President Richard Nixon and his administration. The embarrassing chapter of American history consisted of wiretapping and espionage, and exposed numerous instances of government corruption and misdoing.

193. In an outrageous accusation that echoes McCarthyism, Rep. Allen West (R-FL) has said that eighty Democrats in the House belong to the Communist party.

194. Spiro Theodore Agnew won the vice presidency with President Richard Nixon in 1968 and throughout his career attacked opponents of the Vietnam War as disloyal, criticized intellectuals and college students for not holding traditional values, and often bashed the media for biased coverage. He was forced to resign in 1973 after evidence of corruption, bribery, and tax evasion during his years in Maryland politics were uncovered.

195. The Republican Minority Whip at the time, Newt Gingrich, and his Republican accomplices tried to embarrass and get rid of Democratic congressmen by

making a dramatic public display of exposing the financial corruption of the House and its bank; however, the plan backfired and no money was actually lost or stolen. In fact, it was revealed that Gingrich himself had been writing bad checks and appropriating funds unethically.

196. The Pakistan-based Bank of Credit and Commerce International (BCCI) had an extensive roster of notorious criminal clientele, including Washington lobbyists with close ties to President George Bush, Sr., but also Manuel Noriega, Osama bin Laden, and Saddam Hussein.

197. George Bush and Ronald Reagan, with the assistance of old friends in the CIA, negotiated with Iran to keep American hostages longer than necessary to further their political plans and release the hostages at a time when it would be most convenient for the Republican party.

198. In 1980, Ronald Reagan had President Jimmy Carter's pre-debate notes stolen to better Reagan's performance in the debate.

199. In 1977, Richard Nixon, in the midst of the Watergate scandal, told the press, "If the President does it, it can't be illegal."

200. Republican smear tactics forced Ross Perot, running as an independent at the time, to drop out of the 1992 presidential election due to a smear campaign that included phony nude photos of his daughter and an attempt to sabotage her impending wedding. After the wedding, Perot reentered the race, splitting votes with George Bush and helping Bill Clinton win the election.

201. The 39th United States Congress, with a Republican majority in both the Senate and the House, proposed the 14th Amendment to the Constitution in 1866, which includes the Equal Protection, Due Process, and Citizenship Clauses to protect the rights of Americans, but especially African Americans after emancipation and during the reconstruction. Of the 14th Amendment cases brought before the prominently Republican Supreme Court between 1890 and 1910, nineteen of them dealt with issues of equality for African Americans and 288 were argued to protect corporations and "corporate personhood."

202. During his presidency, Republican Teddy Roosevelt took a hard stand against corporations and monopolies, including bigwigs like Rockefeller, Carnegie, and J. P. Morgan, earning him the nickname "Trust-buster." Infuriated, the GOP rejected Roosevelt from the party, causing him to run on the Progressive Bull Moose ticket in the election of 1912, splitting the conservative vote and allowing Democrat Woodrow Wilson to win the presidency.

203. Almost immediately after becoming president, Gerald Ford pardoned former president Richard Nixon—who had appointed Ford as his vice president resulting in his ascension to president when Nixon himself resigned—before he could be impeached for his involvement in the Watergate scandal and charged with any crimes.

204. George H. W. Bush's grandfather, the late Senator Prescott Bush, had made business dealings with the financial backers of Nazi Germany. The Bush fortune, worth upwards from $1.5 million, had been entwined with that

of Hitler's party until the 1942 Trading with the Enemy Act and the connection had been kept secret until two former slave laborers at Auschwitz brought charges and civil action against the Bush family in 2002.

205. When former New York City Mayor Rudy Giuliani spoke at a tsunami relief charity event in 2005, he charged a speaking fee of $100,000, reportedly more than the event made for the charity itself.

206. While persistently operating under the pretense of being the party of values and morality, the Republican party has amounted innumerable deviant scandals while simultaneously chastising the American people. Some notable scandals include: Republican Senator from Idaho Larry Craig's 2007 arrest for soliciting sex from a male officer in a bathroom stall, after supporting the Federal Marriage Amendment barring extension of rights to same-sex couples; Republican Rep from Florida Mark Foley's resignation after news got out that he'd been using an instant messaging program to send sexually-explicit messages to male pages, one of whom was underage; and the Bush administration and Defense Secretary Donald Rumsfeld's authorization and cover up of cases of sexual assault against Iraqi children in order to humiliate their parents into providing information to the U.S. military.

207. Nelson Rockefeller: "Take the average person, who makes $100,000 a year…"

208. Florida state law prevents anyone with a felony on his/her record from voting. According to Michael Moore, in preparation for the 2000 presidential election, thousands of names were removed from the voter rolls for

simply being similar to the names of felons. In other words, thousands of eligible voters were stricken from the records by Florida Governor Jeb Bush and Florida Secretary of State Katherine Harris.

209. RNC Chairman Michael Steele said of his party in 2009: "You have absolutely no reason, none, to trust our word or our actions at this point."

210. In 1992 members of the House were charged with bouncing checks from the accounts they held with the "House Bank." The worst offender was Tommy Robinson (R-AK), who reportedly overdrew funds 996 times.

211. George Bush: "Rarely is the question asked, 'Is our children learning?'" Bush has a point here, as Al Franken notes. It seems unlikely that this particular question has ever been asked before.

212. Bush: "The reason I believe in a large tax cut is because it's what I believe."

213. Eleven Republicans in Congress voted *against* emergency aid being sent to New Orleans after Hurricane Katrina.

214. The conservative U.S. Supreme Court ruled that officials would be permitted to strip-search anyone arrested for any reason, even if there was no reason to believe that contraband was being held on their person.

215. From 2003 to 2005, Jeff Gannon (not his real name), a conservative reporter who wrote articles for GOPUSA. com and had White House credentials, was frequently

called upon by Press Secretary Scott McClellan to lob softball questions (in one instance, asking a throwaway question studded with the comment that Democrats had "divorced themselves from reality") that raised suspicions that he was planted there to state conservative dogma rather than investigate stories.

216. In 2004, Majority Leader Tom DeLay (R-TX) was rebuked by the House ethics committee for telling Representative Nick Smith (R-MI) that he would endorse Smith's son's congressional bid in exchange for Smith's vote for the Republican-led bill to add prescription drug coverage to Medicare. The scramble for the Republican bill had already undergone the embarrassment of extending the roll call for nearly three hours prior to this scandal.

217. When John McCain accepted the GOP's nomination for president in 2008, the backdrop was an image of Walter Reed Middle High School, without consent from the principal. It's safe to say the school was not the desired image or message of the event, and it was meant instead to be an image of Walter Reed Medical Center, the now-closed army hospital, which would be more in line with McCain's past injuries from the Vietnam War. The hospital underwent much criticism when cases of neglect, bureaucratic red tape, mold, and even cockroaches were occurring in building 18 of the complex; Bush quickly sent an investigation to correct this, but the scandal and the mix-up of images don't reflect well on Republican politicians for staying on top of their affairs, at least related to the medical center intended for American soldiers injured in the foreign wars Republicans are so eager to support.

218. At the 1988 Republican National Convention, George H. W. Bush accepted the party's nomination with an infamous speech containing an even more infamous one-liner: "Read my lips: no new taxes." His lips lied.

219. Former Republican Treasurer Catalina Vasquez Villalpando, appointed by President George H. W. Bush, became the first and only U.S. treasurer to be sent to prison in 1994 when she was convicted of evading federal income taxes, obstructing a corruption investigation, and conspiring with her former company.

220. In 2002, Republican Congressman Gary Miller made over $10 million by selling 165 acres of land to the city of Monrovia, California. Normally there would be a 31 percent tax on this sale, but Miller claimed that Monrovia forced him to sell the land. This claim was later proved to be false, as Miller was the one pursuing the sale.

221. In 2005, Congressman Gary Miller (R-CA) recommended adding language to a transportation bill to close the Rialto airport, which would let the Lewis Operating Corporation redevelop the land. Coincidentally, this company gave $8,100 to Miller's campaign.

Reagan(omics)

222. In 1980, Reagan falsely told America that dramatic tax cuts for the rich would stimulate the economy. Reagan and the right-wing Republicans also assured Americans that cuts to government spending would benefit the United States. However, the promised increase in revenue never came and the deficit skyrocketed. Reagan's trickle-down strategy has also been blamed for increased homelessness and urban decay.

223. Before Reagan's time in office, America's middle class was thriving. However, Reagan's union busting and the creation of corporate incentives robbed the middle class of power, influence, and money. Twelve years of Reaganomics brought down the middle class, consumer spending, and, ultimately, the American economy.

224. On Reagan's watch the debt ballooned from some $700 million to approaching $3 trillion. Reagan himself said the debt was his "greatest disappointment."

225. In 1981, Reagan fired every worker in the air traffic controllers union (PATCO) who had refused his order to return to work. The union had been on strike only two days, and Reagan declared the strike illegal. Reagan's campaign was largely backed by right-wing Christians and Wall Street magnates, who were against unions. Reagan took the PATCO strike as an opportunity to communicate to the American middle class that he was not in their corner.

226. In August 1974, Ronald Regan, a long time Nixon defender, admonishes Nixon and admits that he deceived the country.

227. President Regan himself admitted that "mistakes were made" in his administration's secret arms deals with Iran in the 1986 Iran-Contra scandal.

228. Though most Republicans look up to Ronald Reagan as a symbol of a president who enacted small government, the Republican hero actually increased the government's involvement in many areas that today's GOP presidential candidates base half their campaigns on opposing. For instance, in 1983 he bailed out Social Security after

a failed attempt to privatize it, he planned to cut the Department of Energy and Education but actually ended up adding one of the most expensive and largest, the Department of Veteran's Affairs.

229. Though Reagan is a role model for many Republicans who follow what they believe is his pro-life stance on abortion, they ignore the fact that in 1967, when he was the governor of California, he signed a bill to liberalize abortion in the state. Later, he came to project the blame onto doctors who had misinterpreted the law. The resources Reagan invested into supporting his anti-abortion stance are unconvincing.

230. Republicans who both idolize Ronald Reagan and support immigration crack-downs might be embarrassed to know that during his presidency, Reagan supported a bill that helped 3 million people and millions of family members gain American residency.

231. Reagan, often admired by Republicans for his honesty, was motivated to violate his own rule not to negotiate with terrorists by his inability to free seven American hostages held by Iranian terrorists in Lebanon. As a result, he shipped arms to Iran and violated the embargo.

232. When Reagan's veto of a comprehensive anti-Apartheid act was overridden by Republican-led Congress in 1986, Senator Lowell P. Weicker, Jr. said, "For this moment, at least, the President has become an irrelevancy to the ideals, heartfelt and spoken, of America."

233. Rush Limbaugh asked, "Where did you get this silly notion that Reagan raised taxes?" An appropriate response would be "history."

234. Edmund Morris recalls Reagan wondering if "the Lord brought down this plague [of AIDS because] illicit sex is against the Ten Commandments."

235. In *Lucy in the Afternoon: An Intimate Memoir of Lucille Ball*, Lucille describes Reagan's alleged UFO sighting when he was governor of California: "After he was elected President, I kept thinking about that event, and wondered if he still would have won if he told everyone that he saw a flying saucer."

236. Reagan wrote while editing his 1987 U.N. Assembly speech, "And toward the end perhaps I still would like my 'fantasy'—how quickly our differences world wide would vanish if creatures from another planet should threaten this world."

237. William Worth Belknap, U.S. Secretary of War under President Grant, was indicted for accepting bribes in exchange for political appointments. In the wake of the scandal, Belknap resigned.

238. In a blatant violation of the separation of church and state as outlined in the first amendment, Republican Alabama Supreme Court Chief Justice Roy Moore had a 3-ton monument representing the Ten Commandments displayed outside the courthouse. When Moore was challenged about this disregard for the separation of church and state, Moore had to be forcibly removed from office.

239. The Sarah PAC, supporting Sarah Palin, is supposed to be "dedicated to building America's future by supporting fresh ideas and candidates." However, Palin, has repeatedly dipped into these funds for her own personal use, including a trip to Disneyland.

During President Bush

240. Having lost the popular vote to Al Gore during the 2000 Presidential election after allegations of vote tampering throughout the state of Florida (then governed by Jeb Bush), George W. Bush was then ruled winner and next president by a conservatively leaning Supreme Court, citing the equal protection clause of the 14th Amendment and a general unwillingness to actually count votes.

241. George W. Bush bankrupted two businesses—Arbusto Oil and Spectrum Energy—and was bailed out by wealthy friends and family members both times. He was also accused of insider trading in 1990 while serving on the board of directors at Harken Energy. *U.S. News and World Report* calls the evidence in support of Bush's insider trading "substantial," but, as his father was in office, the SEC exonerated Bush without even interviewing him.

242. Paul Krugman of the *New York Times* suggests that "Bush did as terrible a job fighting terrorism as he did responding to Katrina ... but on the terrorism front, and even in Iraq, the administration could invent a reality that impressed the public."

243. The well-founded implication that president George W. Bush's response to the Hurricane Katrina catastrophe was based on racism has been cited by the president as representing "an all-time low" of his presidency.

244. Bush's vice president, Dick Cheney, was reported to have urged utility companies to divert power away from the Katrina-ravished region during rescue operations to electrical substations in nearby Collins, Mississippi, that were essential to the operation of the Colonial Pipeline, which carries gasoline and diesel fuel from Texas to the Northeast.

245. The Department of Homeland Security, established by President Bush in the wake of the September 11th attacks with the primary responsibilities of protecting the United States from and responding to terrorist attacks, man-made accidents, and natural disasters, exposed its weaknesses and incompetence with a notably lackluster response to Hurricane Katrina due to confusion over authority and general lack of consideration for the event.

246. Following 9/11, President Bush called for wiretapping of certain phone calls without warrants for the sake of national security. Bush was supported in this reprehensible act by Congress, contending that the president was invading citizens' privacy in an attempt to keep Americans safe.

247. Because Bush walked away from the Kyoto Protocol, progress for the international movement to fight climate change has been stilted.

248. President Bush voted early in his Presidency to restrict stem cell research, which has been successful in the treatment of illnesses such as Parkinson's disease.

249. President Bush gave the wealthiest Americans tremendous tax cuts based on the belief that they would take their money to tax shelters abroad. The move concretely disproves the trickle down theory, as the U.S. economy then slid into a recession.

250. America lost 2,910,000 private-sector jobs while Bush was in office.

251. President Bush's record for job creation ranks among the worst since the government began keeping records.

252. Ronald Reagan's famous decision to cut taxes in the 1980s came at a time when the middle class was being lifted into higher tax brackets by inflation. Financial markets had been experiencing little growth for fifteen years, and income equality was falling. In other words, his economic policy was appropriate for the nation at the time and arguably produced results during his presidency. When George W. Bush entered office in 2001, the economic climate was in total opposition to that of the 1980s, but Bush offered the same financial policy. Clearly, Bush's fiscal strategy was not beneficial to the United States.

253. President Bush fired economic advisers for warning of impending economic disaster. Paul O'Neill was fired from the Treasury because he cautioned the president about deficits, and Larry Lindsey was fired from his position as top White House economic adviser for predicting

that cost of the Iraq war would be $200 billion—much higher than the White House's projections.

254. While President Bush's increases in spending and drastic tax cuts may not be responsible for the current economic crisis, they did indeed signify a return to permanent deficits for the United States which leaves the Federal Government much less able to pull the nation out of its economic hardships.

255. In 2001, Bush refused to back the Kyoto Protocol a piece of international legislation placing limits on carbon dioxide and other greenhouse gas emissions. This is but one example of his tendency to choose energy corporations over environmentalists throughout his presidency.

256. Paul Wolfowitz, former president of the World Bank and deputy defense secretary in the George W. Bush White House, used his position to promote and give a raise to Shaha Riza, a bank employee who was his long-term girlfriend, who would be paid more than Condoleeza Rice with the raise. While his office claimed that the Bank's Ethics Committee approved the irregular promotion, Ethics claimed they knew nothing of it. Said Government Accountability Project's international director Beatrice Edwards, "It's ironic that Mr. Wolfowitz lectures developing countries about good governance and fighting corruption, while winking at an irregular promotion and overly generous pay increases to a partner,"

257. Once Bush insider Paul Wolfowitz became president of the World Bank, Republicans were able to push

their social agenda on the international organization. Under Wolfowitz, World Bank started scaling back their long-standing tradition of supporting family planning. Madagascar country program coordinator Lilia Burunciuc wrote to colleagues on March 8, 2007: "One of the requests received from the MD [managing director Juan Jose Daboub] was to take out all references to family planning. We did that." World Bank went on to cut funding for abortion and contraceptives, pushing abstinence programs instead.

258. Under Bush's administration following the 2001 rejection of a proposal to reform the college student loan industry, the Department of Education went suspiciously easy on the $85-billion-a-year student loan industry, which often involves bribing universities with financial incentives if they promote certain student loan companies. Barmak Nasirian, a longtime advocate for industry reform at the American Association of Collegiate Registrars and Admissions Officers, said, "The Department of Education has been run as a wholly owned subsidiary of the loan industry under this administration. They are running the federal loan program for the profit of their friends and not for the benefit of students and taxpayers."

259. Karl Rove and the Bush Administration pushed the issue of voter fraud and claimed that illegal immigrants and deceased people were voting rampantly in U.S. elections. They were so desperate to found this claim that they had the Election Assistance Commission alter its report to emphasize the issue and downplay proof of exaggeration. The original report said that among experts "there

is widespread but not unanimous agreement that there is little polling place fraud," but the final version that was released to the public said in its executive summary that "there is a great deal of debate on the pervasiveness of fraud."

260. Also caught in the wake of the Bush Administration's push to argue for widespread voter fraud were several U.S. attorneys who were fired in December 2006, because they were told by the White House to search out cases of voter fraud that the attorneys did not think warranted so much attention, and thus they did not fulfill the request.

261. The Department of Education under the Bush Administration paid nationally syndicated commentator Armstrong Williams $240,000 in taxpayer money so he would promote the No Child Left Behind Act.

262. In 2002, syndicated columnist Maggie Gallagher repeatedly promoted President George W. Bush's $300 million initiative to encourage marriage as a way of strengthening families. She did not mention that she had a $21,500 contract with the Department of Health and Human Services to do so. When the scandalous link was revealed, Gallagher apologized to readers, saying "I should have disclosed a government contract when I later wrote about the Bush marriage initiative. I would have, if I had remembered it."

263. A third columnist on the federal payroll under the Bush Administration was Michael McManus, a marriage advocate who wrote a syndicated column, "Ethics & Religion." He was hired as a subcontractor by the

Department of Health and Human Services to promote Bush's marriage initiative, but did not disclose this fact to his readers. He received $10,000 for his efforts.

264. Rep. Louise Slaughter (D-N.Y.) sent a letter to President Bush to assert that his "Administration has, on several occasions, paid members of the media to advocate in favor of Administration policies."

265. During the Bush Administration, the Center for Media and Democracy revealed that fifty-four "video news releases" (VNRs) that were produced by the government were used by forty-six news stations without disclosing that these were government commercials, not news. Publicists posing as journalists were used by the Department of Health and Human Services to promote the Medicare expansion bill.

266. When confronted with the issue of these misleading VNRs, former President Bush said, "Yes, it's deceptive to the American people if it's not disclosed" that the government was the source of the "news" segments. However, the government news releases are often cheap and satisfy the cost-cutting demands of news programs. While Bush's Administration was successful at getting their news releases broadcast, Bush blamed the broadcasters and not the government producers for the misleading lack of disclosure.

267. Karl Rove deleted emails sent from his Republican National Committee email address and claimed that he believed, contrary to RNC's policy, that the emails were automatically saved and his deletions wouldn't matter. However, the lost emails are estimated at

5 million, and they might have contained valuable information regarding the suspicious firing of U.S. attorneys during the Bush Administration. Sen. Patrick Leahy (D-VT), the chairman of the Senate Judiciary Committee said, "You can't erase e-mails, not today. They've gone through too many servers. They can't say they've been lost. That's like saying, 'The dog ate my homework.'

268. Bush-appointed Food and Drug Administration Commissioner Lester Crawford resigned in 2005 after pleading guilty to conflict of interest and false reporting for owning stocks that he oversaw at the FDA. He made $39,000 from the tainted stocks.

269. Attorney General Alberto R. Gonzales at first denied allegations that the U.S. attorneys he fired were let go because of political reasons and not performance-related ones. However, when the truth came out that they were fired for not taking enough voter fraud cases to support the Bush Administration's cause of exaggerating voter fraud's threat, Gonzales was told by many to step down, which he refused to do. (He did admit the firings were "flawed" but wished to keep his own job.)

270. During the 2006 midterm elections, members of the Bush administration were found to be using taxpayer funds to campaign for Republican candidates.

271. President Bush famously said, "You are either with us or against us." This statement is a fitting characterization of the Republican unwillingness to compromise and seek bipartisan agreements.

272. In 2003, the Bush administration leaked the covert status of Agent Valerie Plame Wilson of the CIA.

273. Karl Rove's protégé Timothy Griffin directed opposition research for the Republican National Committee for the Bush campaign during the 2004 election. Griffin accidentally sent a "caging list" to the wrong email address and inadvertently revealed a list of 1,886 names and addresses of traditionally Democrat and predominantly African American areas of Jacksonville, Florida. The state allows political party operatives to keep voters from obtaining ballots and slow the voting process, as Griffin appeared to be planning. Mindy Tucker Fletcher, Florida's republican state campaign spokeswoman, did not deny that the list was intended to challenge certain voters (including African American soldiers, minorities, and poor voters) on Election Day.

274. The removal of H.E. "Bud" Cummins III from the position of U.S. attorney in Arkansas and the act of replacing him with Timothy Griffin: special assistant to Bush, Karl Rove's deputy, and GOP political operative. When it was found that the firing and replacement were motivated by partisan rather than policy reasons, Griffin resigned from the position rather than facing a Senate confirmation.

CHAPTER FOUR

WAR

Throughout the history of our country, we have only not been at war for a total of fifty-eight years. Fifty-eight years! That is an absolutely staggering statistic. Today, we have soldiers stationed around the world, fighting for "freedom." Unfortunately, we are obsessed with spreading democracy around the world, and every day, American soldiers are losing their lives. We invaded Iraq to destroy their 'weapons of mass destruction,' but the only problem was that they didn't have any. Republicans are so obsessed with war, but it's interesting that most of them have never served their country. They're quick to send over someone else's children to fight, but we doubt they'd let their own children.

Given the current state of this country, it is obvious that we should be spending the majority of our time improving the standard of living for Americans. We see ourselves as a superpower that should be helping less fortunate countries but the problem is that things aren't going swimmingly here. The country is in debt, the economy is in the toilet, unemployment is rising by the day, and these Republicans want to keep spending our money to fight battles in other places! Don't they realize that *we* need that money!

Also, think about the troops who signed up to defend this country, and are doing anything but that. What are they fighting for? So that we can improve another country, when the one they're protecting is in crisis?

Now, we at PDR are all for spreading democracy and improving the way of life for those less fortunate; but only under the conditions that the way of life in our country is up to code and that the American people are prospering.

We are not.

It'd be nice if all the money spent spreading democracy would be used to improve our democracy, but as you'll see from the Republican Party, that's far from what they'd like to do.

War on Terror

275. The Bush administration's post-September 11, 2001 war on terror has created a "culture of fear" in this country, according to Washington Post columnist Zbigniew Brzezinski. The phrase war on terror "has actually undermined our ability to effectively confront the real challenges we face from fanatics who may use terrorism against us."

276. Corporations have used the war on terror to swindle billions of dollars in tax cuts and government sponsored incentives by presenting private defense and energy programs to Republican politicians that threaten the environment and may actually weaken national security.

277. The Patriot Act, which was enacted in the immediate wake of the September 11th attacks to supposedly provide the tools necessary for the government to prevent terrorism while limiting the rights of Americans, was written and prepared long before the attack occurred.

278. In fact, the similarly worded 1996 Antiterrorism Act, which would five years later prove to be completely

ineffective in protecting the country from terrorism, espoused principles that were regarded as fundamentally unconstitutional.

279. Besides there not being much evidence to conclude that these sorts of laws actually prevented terrorism, the administrations of Reagan, Bush Sr., and eventually Bush Jr. pushed for legislation that would limit the rights of citizens and cleverly circumvent the constitution so as to reinstate 1950s anti-communist scare tactics.

280. Republicans Newt Gingrich, Mitt Romney, Michele Bachmann, Herman Cain, and Rick Santorum have all, on various occasions, declared the United States to be at war—justifying the use of the Patriot Act and the abuses of power therein—but rarely referred to the specific wars in Afghanistan or Iraq that President Obama has made attempts to bring to a close; the implication being that the country is in a constant state of war and the Patriot Act and war ideology is here to stay.

281. The Authorization for the Use of Military Force (AUMF) passed by Congress three days after September 11, 2001 to give President Bush the power to use military force to seek justice for the attacks has recently been scrutinized by House Republicans for not being enough to fight potential terrorist threats when all those that contributed to the attacks on 9-11 have been brought to justice. Rep. Mac Thornberry (R-Texas) and Rep. Mckeon (R-Calif.) have suggested removing from the language of the updated proposal any reference to 9/11 and adding more generic anti-terrorist language.

282. House Republicans included in a proposed 2012 authorization bill a section essentially declaring a permanent war against unnamed Taliban and al Qaeda operatives and ambiguous, indirectly related, terror groups, despite House Democrat's opposition.

283. The Republican party started the costly war in Iraq under the auspices of Iraq and Saddam Hussein being a threat to national security, but tend to blame any apparent setback or potential defeat on the Democrats, a tradition established heartily by Richard Nixon.

284. Representative Patrick McHenry (R-NC) did not serve in any war or in the military at all, but saw it fit to break military protocol and endanger the lives of soldiers by giving away sensitive information that led to one of the deadliest attacks on the Green Zone in recent years, during his visit to Iraq.

285. The list of Republican politicians that have expressed pro-war sentiments but have avoided and dodged actual service is long and extensive but includes: former VP Dick Cheney (several deferments); Bush advisor Karl Rove (draft dodger); former Speaker Newt Gingrich (draft dodger); both Bush boys, Jeb and George W., have avoided active duty (George got out of his National Guard commitment 2 years early and Jeb never served); and former Gov. Arnold Schwarzenegger (went AWOL from his Austrian army base to enter a bodybuilding competition).

286. Michele Bachmann blamed President Obama for the $805 billion spent and 4,400 American lives lost in the war in Iraq. However, when discussing this in an interview

with CNN's Wolf Blitzer, she failed to acknowledge Bush's responsibility for starting that war when Blitzer pointed out that the Iraq War "started in March 2003 – that was President Bush and the Republicans who launched that war that went on for years. This current president is now withdrawing all of those troops from Iraq."

287. Reviewing Dick Cheney's book *In My Time*, Paul A. Gigot writes, "Mr. Cheney doesn't say this directly, but it's clear that this failure to settle disputes contributed greatly to the post-invasion troubles in Iraq. Mr. Bush was too loyal for too long to too many aides who gave him bad advice and even worked against his own policies."

288. Until George W. Bush's administration, "enhanced techniques" of torture had never come into play in discussions of war strategies. Cheney downplays these techniques in his memoir *In My Time* by making the definition of torture unclear, calling it instead "interrogation techniques that human rights groups claim constitute torture." But waterboarding, stress positions, sleep deprivation, and other unethical techniques are no way to win a war, as history has shown.

289. Under George W. Bush, the White House asked at least twice if CIA officials could dig up information to discredit Juan Cole, a professor at the University of Michigan whose influential blog criticized the war in Iraq, according to Glenn L. Carle, a former Central Intelligence Agency officer who was a top counterterrorism official at the time.

290. Dick Cheney: "I was a big supporter of waterboarding."

291. In regards to wartime waterboarding, both Herman Cain and Michele Bachmann have come out in support, despite several military leaders emphatically rejecting the tactic and other forms of torture. Cain has even said, "I don't see it as torture. I see it as an enhanced-interrogation technique."

292. Bush administration officials, Dick Cheney in particular, have asserted that waterboarding and general torture of captured soldiers has provided the military with important intelligence, but no evidence has been provided to support the claim.

293. In his memoir, President George W. Bush reveals that the CIA submitted a list of interrogation techniques and he chose waterboarding as an interrogation technique for terror suspects, suggesting, as a defense, that there were two worse torture techniques that he turned down.

294. Republicans have shown disapproval of both Obama's and Bush's release of prisoners from the Guantanamo Bay prison in Cuba, claiming that both administrations placed desire to earn goodwill internationally and placate domestic pressures above torturing terror suspects, imprisoning them indefinitely, and ignoring human rights violations.

295. While Democrats debate if and how to close the prison, Congressional Republicans are generally united in their stance on keeping Guantanamo open indefinitely, stoking the fears of the American people of having detainees released to the U.S. mainland. Rep Todd Tiahrt of Kansas has even proposed a bill to disallow

tax payer funds going to relocation of detainees from Guantanamo to the mainland.

296. The Guantanamo Bay detention center, which the Republicans want so badly to remain open and refitted partly by Halliburton defense contractors, was an attempt by the U.S. government to circumvent U.S. and international law, and the prison has become internationally recognized for gross human rights abuses perpetrated by the U.S.

297. Human rights violations performed by the United States military on both Iraqi citizens and soldiers at the Abu Ghraib prison—including physical, psychological, and sexual abuse, torture, sodomy, and homicide—were brought to light in 2004 with photographic evidence and first-person reports. Although the Bush administration claim the injustices were uncharacteristic of U.S. actions during the wars in Iraq and Afghanistan, organizations like the International Committee of the Red Cross (ICRC) argue that the techniques and treatment of prisoners at Abu Ghraib are consistent with American international reputation in military conflict dating back to Vietnam. Republican Former Secretary of Defense Rumsfeld allegedly even approved many of the heinous actions carried out in Abu Ghraib and throughout the war.

298. The Bush administration thoroughly defused the Abu Ghraib atrocities by minimizing the appearance of damage in the public eye—a large amount incriminating evidence was classified as items of national security and kept away from the media and American people; General Taguba's report was intentionally focused on the events surrounding the photos that were already

uncovered and not any larger misconduct—a Pentagon consultant claimed that the administration's plan was to "prosecute the kids in the photographs but protect the big picture"; and lastly, the administration performed a widespread media attack on all critics, using Abu Ghraib to depict Democrats as anti-American and unpatriotic.

299. Some supporters of former president George W. Bush credit the death of Osama bin Laden in May 2011 to Bush rather than to President Obama. Many Republican politicians issued statements reacting to bin Laden's death that either did not mention Obama or credited him only with following the leadership of Bush.

300. When Osama bin Laden was captured and killed in May 2011, House Majority Leader Eric Cantor (R-VA) said, "I commend President Obama who has followed the vigilance of President Bush in bringing bin Laden to justice."

301. Newt Gingrich also played down the significance of President Obama's leadership when he reacted to Osama bin Laden's death. "I commend both President George W. Bush who led the campaign against our enemies … and President Obama who continued and intensified the campaign in both Afghanistan and Pakistan," said Gingrich.

302. A counterterrorism official in September 2006 said, "The handful of assets we have have given us nothing close to real-time intelligence" that could help U.S. intelligence find and kill Osama bin Laden. Under Bush's presidency, the trail to take out bin Laden had gone "stone cold."

303. In a discussion on Fox News where *Weekly Standard* editor Fred Barnes explained his meeting with Bush in the Oval Office in September 2006, Barnes said that Bush told him finding Osama bin Laden was "not a top priority use of American resources" and that Bush "says, you know, getting Osama bin Laden is a low priority."

304. *Weekly Standard* editor Fred Barnes met with Bush in the Oval Office in September 2006 and reported on the *Weekly Standard* blog that Bush's message was that capturing "bin Laden doesn't fit with the administration's strategy for combating terrorism."

305. A 2009 Senate Foreign Relations Committee report reveals that Bush shifted his focus away from capturing Osama bin Laden just as he was "within our grasp": "For critics of the Bush administration's commitment to Afghanistan, the shift in focus just as Franks and his senior aides were literally working on plans for the attacks on Tora Bora represents a dramatic turning point that allowed a sustained victory in Afghanistan to slip through our fingers."

306. A 2009 Senate Foreign Relations Committee "report removes any lingering doubts and makes it clear that Osama bin Laden was within our grasp [during the Bush administration] at Tora Bora....The information comes from U.S. military officers at Tora Bora, from detainees who were in the camps with bin Laden, from the senior CIA officer in Afghanistan at the time, and from the official history of the special operations forces. Based on that evidence, it is clear that the Al Qaeda leader was within reach of U.S. troops three months after the attacks on New York and Washington."

307. Michael Scheuer, a former senior CIA. official who was the first head of the Alec Station unit responsible for hunting Osama bin Laden, claimed that the decision to close the unit in 2006 and shift focus away from bin Laden as a threat during the Bush administration would "clearly denigrate our operations against Al Qaeda."

308. Lt. Col. Reid Sawyer, the director of the Combating Terrorism Center at West Point, told NPR in May 2011 that had Bush's administration succeeded in killing bin Laden eight years ago in Tora Bora, al-Qaida might not have been able to recover. But now he worries that the terrorist organization could easily bounce back after years to prepare for bin Laden's death.

309. In the budget, Bush and the Republicans ignored the conservatively estimated $3 trillion cost of the two Bush wars. The Congressional Budget Office's estimate was about a trillion or two.

310. The budget deficits under President Bush are mostly a result of the cost of the U.S. occupation of Iraq, a trillion (according to the Bush administration) or three (according to Linda Bilmes and Joseph Stiglitz). What benefits to the U.S. were worth this cost?

311. Dan Bartlett, former Bush White House Communicators Director and Counselor to the President, said, "We strongly believe that terrorists picked up off the battlefield ... do not qualify for protections under Geneva. Five members of the Supreme Court disagreed. As the president said, we will comply with the ruling."

312. David Remes, a lawyer who represents seventeen Yemeni detainees at Guantanamo Bay, said in 2006 that

"the legal architecture of the war on terror was built on a foundation of unlimited and unaccountable presidential power, including the power to decide unilaterally whether, when and to whom to apply the Geneva Conventions."

313. "Had I known there was going to be an attack on America, I would have moved mountains to stop the attack. And had there been actionable intelligence, we would have moved on it," Bush said.

314. "I never saw any intelligence that indicated there was going to be an attack on America—at a time and a place, an attack," Bush told reporters. "Had I known there was going to be an attack on America, I would have moved mountains to stop the attack. And had there been actionable intelligence, we would have moved on it." On August 6, 2001, while Bush was vacationing at his ranch in Texas, he received a memo from the CIA entitled "Bin Ladin Determined to Strike in US."

315. George W. Bush unfurled a "Mission Accomplished" banner in May 2003 to declare victory in Iraq.

316. According to a BBC News article on September 16, 2004: "The United Nations Secretary-General Kofi Annan has told the BBC the US-led invasion of Iraq was an illegal act that contravened the UN charter."

317. In 2003, only one day after the forty-eight-hour ultimatum was issued to Saddam Hussein to leave Iraq, Colin Powell announced that the Bush administration would lead a "coalition of the willing" to liberate Iraq. However, the UN considers this impatient decision to be illegal.

318. Once George W. Bush got rid of Saddam Hussein, his lack of planning for Iraq after achieving this goal caused many issues in the destabilized country. The results of this situation, besides the large amount of money spent on it, include thousands of soldier casualties, and an unknown number of civilian casualties as well.

319. Arthur Keller, veteran CIA case officer working for the Iraq Survey Group, discussed Bush's failed attempt to support his case for war based on the threat of Saddam Hussein's alleged weapons of mass destruction: "The CIA accomplished something of a mission impossible: proving a negative. In candid moments, most of the group's members had quietly acknowledged by late 2003 that Iraq had no banned weapons for us to find. But we kept searching for another year, until shortly after the November 2004 U.S. elections.... Given the perennial shortage of CIA case officers, the Bush administration's insistence on keeping the Iraq Survey Group open meant that other crucial work didn't get done."

320. In 2006, Brit Hume of Fox News reported, ignoring evidence to the contrary, that "[t]op administration officials said today that chemical and biological weapons have indeed been found in Iraq." John Gibson and Jim Angle at Fox, in addition to nationally syndicated radio hosts Rush Limbaugh and Janet Parshall, also spread the false news of weapons of mass destruction. But CNN national security correspondent David Ensor told the missing piece of this story soon after: "Charles Duelfer, the CIA's weapons inspector, tells us the weapons are all pre-Gulf War vintage shells, no longer effective weapons. Not evidence, he says, of an ongoing WMD program under Saddam Hussein."

321. Typically, when a nation is at war, taxes rise. This helps pay for military efforts and also shows national solidarity with the troops—as many Presidents have noted, it seems wrong to profit while men and women are risking their lives. However, Bush continued to cut taxes after sending the country to war. Perhaps the war in Iraq would have been more popular had President Bush's economic policy encouraged unity with the men and women fighting it.

322. While the majority of Americans supported President Obama's move to pull all American troops out of Iraq by the end of 2011, Republicans continually criticize this action, preferring instead to have kept thousands of American troops stranded in Iraq indefinitely.

323. For years, Republican rhetoric—parroted by the likes of George W. Bush, Dick Cheney, Sarah Palin, and John McCain, to name a few—insisted that the War on Terror was necessitated by 9/11 and was the price Americans had to pay for their freedom. However, connections between the 9/11 attack and Iraq or between al-Qaeda and Saddam Hussein have never been proven.

324. Hans Blix, an international lawyer and former UN chief weapons inspector has called the Iraq war illegal.

325. A study by a nonprofit journalism organization found that the Bush administration lied about the War on Terror 935 times between 2001 and 2003.

326. The same study found that Bush and administrative officials said definitively (but falsely) that Iraq had weapons of mass destruction 532 times in two years.

327. The War on Terror actually increased the number of jihadist terrorist attacks globally. The yearly incidence of attacks rose 607 percent, and the fatality rate rose 237 percent after the United States became involved in Iraq.

328. The U.S. invasion of Iraq was also detrimental to Iraqis. In 2006, a reported 30 percent of Iraqi children attended school, while before the war the rate was close to 100 percent.

329. While it is nearly impossible to precisely enumerate all Iraqi civilian casualties, the death toll is estimated to be between 50,000 and 100,000, with some estimates as high as 600,000.

330. In 2007, Army suicide rates were higher than they had been in nearly thirty years. About 25 percent of these deaths occurred in Iraq, and many blame the U.S. invasion of Iraq for this sad statistic.

331. A reported 20 percent of soldiers in Iraq and Afghanistan had to be medicated for depression while deployed.

332. In 2007, a reported $6 billion worth of military con-tracts in Kuwait, Iraq, and Afghanistan were being reviewed by criminal investigators.

333. The Iraq war cost a reported $1 trillion, and $9 billion of taxpayer dollars go unaccounted for to this day.

334. Senate Majority Leader Harry Reid reported that the war in Iraq spent $5,000 every second in 2008.

335. Congresswoman Maxine Waters (D-CA) replied in 2007 when asked what message it might send if U.S. troops "cut and run": "Well, I think cut and run is a kind of

language that has been used by this administration and others to intimidate those of us who are responding to the American people's desire to get our soldiers out of Iraq. Our soldiers are dying every day. Civilians are dying by the thousands—uh, in Iraq. I just don't want to wake up one morning to find that they have bombed one of our compounds and hundreds of our soldiers have been killed."

336. President Bush: "I like to tell people when the final history is written on Iraq, it [the bloodshed] will look like just a comma."

337. Rarely did Bush's administration give clear and consistent reasons for U.S. involvement in Iraq. As one example, Condoleeza Rice noted in 2002 that investigations concerning a "nuclear weapons program" were being performed. However, in 2006, she said plainly, "We are there because we are trying to—having overthrown a brutal dictator who was a destabilizing force in the Middle East—we're trying to help the Iraqis create a stable foundation for democracy and a stable foundation for peace."

338. Critics of the Abu Ghraib scandal wondered whether then-Defense Secretary Donald Rumsfeld knew about the extremely inhumane torture practices going on before the press did, as Rumsfeld twice offered his resignation to Bush but the president didn't accept it.

339. After 9/11, the Bush Administration pushed for wiretaps without warrants. The September 11th Advocates, a group of relatives of the victims of the 2001 attacks, issued a news release alleging that the "Bush administration has continually used 9/11 as an excuse to break the laws of our great nation."

340. Former chief of staff to Cheney, I. Lewis "Scooter" Libby, Jr. was convicted March 6, 2007, of lying to FBI agents and grand jurors about a lapse in memory regarding unmasking the classified status of Valerie Plame. Plame is the wife of Joe Wilson, a political opponent to "Scooter" Libby because he disputed President Bush's State of the Union claim that Iraq had sought uranium from Niger.

341. While American lives are at stake with the decision to go to war, Republican Vice President Dick Cheney's former company Halliburton was profiting. Cheney made $34 million from Halliburton's involvement in Iraq.

342. The Defense budget proposed by Republicans for 2013 is especially large, but, like all Defense spending, the real number is actually significantly larger—including supplementary budgets that are rarely made public, "overseas contingency operations" budgets, nuclear weapons development, military retirement costs, and so forth—according to a former Senate staffer at the Center for Defense Information, Winslow Wheeler. The number is often more than $1 trillion, despite the much lower number indicated by the GOP.

343. On May 2, 2007, Rep. John Shimkus (R-IL) compared the war in Iraq to a baseball rivalry. On the House floor, he said to fellow Congress members, "Imagine my beloved St. Louis Cardinals are playing the much despised Chicago Cubs."

War on Drugs

344. In 1914, Dr. Hamilton Wright, appointed by Republican President Teddy Roosevelt, testified before

Congress that drugs made Blacks uncontrollable and prone to rape, and were primarily being consumed by "degenerate Mexicans" and "Chinamen," despite the statistics telling that the majority of users and addicts of opiates and cocaine at the time were white female housewives. This led to Congress passing the Harrison Narcotics Act, one of the earliest acts of federal drug regulation.

345. The war on drugs has been prominent in the Republican camp since President Richard Nixon used "drugs" as coded propaganda for his prejudice against minorities and hippies.

346. In the 1980s, President Ronald Reagan first coined the phrase "war on drugs" while Nancy Reagan, the first lady, led a "Just Say No" campaign against drugs that equated use with immorality.

347. Congress passed the Anti-Drug Abuse Act of 1986 with the urging of Reagan and initiated a three-fold attack on drugs and the American citizen: prominent workplace drug testing; forced education and rehabilitation; and greater military and police involvement up and down the chain of trafficking.

348. President George Bush, Sr. followed suit in the war on drugs—despite evidence that Reagan had been losing the war—with another Anti-Drug Abuse Act in 1988 and the creation of a cabinet-level drug czar position, held first by gambling addict William Bennett (who allegedly lost millions of dollars in Las Vegas on an evening in 2003).

349. Pres. George W. Bush, a staunch advocate for the war on drugs, slyly acknowledged using marijuana in the

past, stating, "I wouldn't answer the marijuana questions. You know why? Because I don't want some little kid doing what I tried."

350. Despite health effects being a large portion of the Republican anti-drug sentiment, Republican lawmakers, like former Senator Strom Thurmond, seem to gladly sacrifice the health of Americans for the benefit of big Tobacco and other corporate interests.

351. Newt Gingrich has even gone on record claiming that anyone responsible for shipping drugs in this country should be put to death, going so far as to sponsor the Drug Importer Death Penalty Act of 1996.

352. More than $51 billion is spent on the war on drugs annually.

353. Drug legalization and taxation at rates comparable to alcohol and tobacco would yield $46.7 billion annually.

354. The number of Americans in prison for drug related offenses has increased 550 percent in the past twenty years, and in 2010 alone, 1,638,846 people were arrested on nonviolent drug charges, 853,838 for marijuana, and 88 percent of that for minor possessions.

355. Two out of three Black or Hispanic Americans are incarcerated for a drug offense annually, despite equal or lower usage rates than their white counterparts. In Chicago, in particular, 55 percent of Black men have been labeled felons due to drug-related charges and are prevented from voting and kept from scholarships and government assistance.

356. Republicans appear hypocritical in their opposition to President Obama's health care plan on the grounds that the government should not have such authority over Americans' health and bodies, while opposing marijuana legalization, especially for medicinal purposes, claiming that the government does, in fact, have that authority.

CHAPTER FIVE

IN BED WITH BIG BUSINESS

The answer to the question, "Why are Republicans always siding with big business?" is actually an easy one. The reason that they always seem to take the side of the gigantic corporations is mainly because they are part of them. Whether they worked for them at one point in their career or through the power elite grew up with the CEO's son, one hand has always been washing the other. You not only see this in the decisions they make, but in the money they receive.

It's no secret that most Republicans were born into wealth. They've grown up sitting side by side with the most powerful people in the country. Seeing as they're "old buddies," it's no surprise that Republicans don't hesitate when giving big business tax breaks or creating financial loopholes.

Here's an interesting fact for you: Did you know that in England, gas is actually more expensive than it is here? Now, you may have indeed known this, but I bet you don't know what happens with that tax money. Well, the money that is made in England from people paying for gas goes to repairing streets, bridges, and other parts of the country. In America, that money goes right into the pockets of the oil companies, while you continue to spend $11 to cross a bridge. Don't you see something wrong with this?

In the book *DemoCRIPS and ReBLOODlicans* by Jesse Ventura and Dick Russell, the former governor lists the Republican candidates up for election and shows their ties to big business. It is absolutely horrifying to see how many of these elected officials have such a heavy bias when it comes to their friends in big business. Once again, rather than these officials looking out for the people who have elected them, they make sure that the first people they take care of are the ones greasing their pockets, and everybody else comes second.

Big Oil: Greasing Republican Pockets

357. According to watchdog groups like Open Secrets and the Sunlight Foundation, some of the larger corporate contributors to the GOP are TRT Holdings, Inc., which gave an estimated $5 million to Republican candidates in 2010; Molson Coors Brewing, which gave more than $107,000 to political campaigns, 95 percent to the GOP; Time Warner, which gave 81 percent of its $983,983 in political contributions to the GOP; and Exxon Mobil, which gave 87 percent of its more than $1 million in political donations to Republican campaigns—all certainly hinting at why the Republicans prefer corporations over people.

358. After significant contributions to Republican campaigns, Exxon is able to limit its tax burden with subsidiaries and operations outside the United States that legally (because of Republican policy) protect the cash flow. So, out of $17.6 billion in taxable income in 2009, Exxon paid none of it to the IRS.

359. In 2010, with the support of 7 Democrats, 234 Republicans in the House of Representatives voted to

block a bill to eliminate a $1.8 billion annual subsidy that treats (foreign) oil drilling as "domestic manufacturing."

360. Despite telling their constituents that they intend to end wasteful, unaffordable, and largely unfair oil subsidies, House Republicans persistently choose to defend them and protect companies such as Exxon Mobil, by far one of the most profitable company on the Forbes Fortune 500 list yearly.

361. In 2012, the top energy/natural resource contributors—Koch Industries, Exxon Mobil, and others like them—gave $31,111,924 to Republican candidates.

362. Oil tycoons such as Jack Gerard, president and chief executive of the American Petroleum Institute trade group, feel so confident about their control of the political system that they threaten "huge electoral consequences" to get their way. Gerard alluded to this when discussing the Keystone XL pipeline and Obama's opposition to it.

363. The amount of fossil fuel/Big Oil funding going to those who voted for the Republican sponsored bill extending a cut in Social Security payroll taxes, which also would fast track a decision on the Keystone XL pipeline and contribute to significantly to environmental pollution, was more than $41 million.

364. The Republicans' twenty-one page manifesto, "Pledge to America," laying out their agenda and promises to the American people, was created largely by a House staffer

who, up until April 2010, served as a lobbyist for some of the nation's most powerful oil, pharmaceutical, and insurance companies.

365. Republican failure to end Big Oil subsidies has driven gas prices up to over $4 per gallon in many areas of the country. ExxonMobil, Shell, Chevron, and ConocoPhillips had profits of $137 billion in 2011, while Americans see rising costs each time they fill their tanks.

366. In 2009, Exxon Mobil paid no federal income taxes. Ninety percent of Exxon's contributions last year went to Republicans.

367. Growth Energy, an ethanol lobbying group, disclosed that Newt Gingrich earned $312,500 as a consultant, when in reality they actually paid Gingrich $600,000.

368. Senator Jim Inhofe (R-OK) has accepted close to $850,000 from ExxonMobil and other oil/gas companies throughout his career.

369. Senator Olympia Snowe (R-ME) has said, "To the average American who's struggling, we're in some other stratosphere. We're the party of Big Business and Big Oil and the rich." However, Big Oil contributed almost $20 billion to the Republican party during the last election, and the securities and investments industry contributed over $54 million. These figures demonstrate that the characterization of the GOP as "the party of Big Business and Big Oil" is—no pun intended—right on the money.

370. Rep. Lee Terry (R-NE) proposed a bill to override Obama and force the rapid approval of the controversial

Keystone pipeline. According to the Dirty Energy Money Campaign, Terry has sided with "dirty energy interests in 100 percent of selected votes. Since 1999, Terry has received $365,798 from the fossil fuel industry, as well as $15,500 from Koch Industries and $25,500 from Exxon Mobil.

371. Senator John Cornyn (R-TX) has "sided with Dirty Energy interests in 100 percent of selected votes" and accepted $2,069,035 from oil and coal companies.

372. Oil Spill Liability legislation would increase liability regarding how much companies are made to pay following an oil spill. Predictably, Republicans shot this bill down.

373. Republicans in Congress blocked legislation imposing a tax on companies sending jobs overseas. The GOP rewards businesses sending jobs out of America with tax breaks.

American Crossroads: Karl Rove's Outside Group as a Meeting of Money and Politics

374. A fellow Republican outside group organizer claimed that "Karl [Rove, former Bush adviser] has always said: People call us a vast right-wing conspiracy, but we're really a half-assed right-wing conspiracy. Now, he wants to get more serious." Rove followed that intention by helping to create American Crossroads, a self-described "grassroots" conservative outside group with $4.7 million, 97 percent of which was contributed by only four billionaires, two of whom are in the oil and gas industry.

375. American Crossroads donor Robert Rowling (worth $4.4 billion) got his start in his father's company, Tana Oil & Gas, and went on to form Chief Oil & Gas. He now owns TRT Holdings, which gave Karl Rove's conservative outside group $1 million. Rowling also contributed $1 million to Progress for America in 2004 to fund the outside group's support for Bush's reelection.

376. Also at the "crossroads" of American Crossroads and Chief Oil & Gas is Trevor Rees-Jones, president of Chief Oil & Gas. Rees-Jones made about $1.5 billion from investing in gas prospects and donated $1 million to American Crossroads. He also gave a total of $38,500 combined to the Texas GOP and John McCain's presidential campaign in 2008.

377. American Crossroads' biggest contributor ($1.55 million) is Bradley Wayne Hughes, chairman of Public Storage Inc. Hughes is worth $3.9 billion and raises thoroughbred horses.

378. The son of the largest American Crossroads donor Bradley Wayne Hughes, B. Wayne Hughes, Jr., is on the board the American Action Network, a conservative front group where a number of executives and lobbyists have a potential interest in rolling back financial regulations.

379. American Crossroads is a legally independent, national political organization operating under special tax laws, charged with helping Republicans win elections by providing significant funding from big business and billionaires with secretive dummy corporations such as Southwest Louisiana Land LLC, owned by billionaire conservative Harold. Simmons

has contributed millions to American Crossroads, to Newt Gingrich's PAC, and to Oliver North's defense fund, and was the sole funder of the slanderous ad campaign in 2008 aimed at linking Obama to Bill Ayers.

380. Wealthy donors have contributed over $30 million to American Crossroads. The group plans to spend over $50 million on ads and other advocacy methods to support the GOP in the 2012 elections.

381. Because American Crossroads has filed with the IRS as a 527 group under the guise of being a grassroots organization, there are no limits to how much money they can collect from the wealthy. Despite claiming it's grassroots, America Crossroads is made for large-scale contributors rather than actual individual donors. Also suspect is the fact that American Crossroads's IRS form lists "no@email" as its email address.

K Street and Lobbyists

382. In 2010, House Speaker-elect John Boehner hired Brett Loper, the medical device industry's chief lobbyist, as his policy director straight from K Street.

383. Many Republican senators have hired lobbyists as top aides. These include Senators Ron Johnson (R-WI), Mike Lee (R-UT), and Rand Paul (R-KY). K Streeters have also been hired by Representatives Robert Dold (R-IL), Steve Pearce (R-NM), and Jeff Denham (R-CA).

Wall Street

384. Republicans are against Wall Street reform and want to repeal Dodd-Frank, a law that created significant

financial regulation to protect consumers and help prevent future financial crises.

385. The Club for Growth intends to raise the next generation of Reagans by threatening Republican politicians against moderate policies. Wall Street high-ups make up much of the membership of Club for Growth. Founder Stephen Moore says that, led by "ideology [rather] than party," CFG thinks it has "an important role in disciplining the party" to align with more hardcore Republican voters.

386. When President George W. Bush took office, the radical Club for Growth founder Stephen Moore said, "Reagan's third term has arrived."

387. Jack Abramoff pleaded guilty in 2006 to conspiracy, fraud, and tax evasion. The "superlobbyist" ripped off Indian-run casinos and bribed Republican leaders in Congress and midlevel officials in the Bush administration. He even gifted former Ohio republican congressman Bob Ney with a golf junket in Scotland. Bush, Tom DeLay, and others involved rushed to give back any contributions obtained from Abramoff.

388. Also involved in Abramoff's lobbying scandal was a long list of Republican politicians: former congressman Robert W. Ney (R-OH); David H. Safavian, former deputy director of the White House Office of Management and Budget; and several former congressional aides who had become lobbyists, including two who had worked for former House majority leader Tom DeLay (R-TX).

389. Once the No. 2 official in the Interior Department, a former mining lobbyist, and a high-level Bush admini-

stration official, J. Steven Griles admitted to hiding his connection with superlobbyist Jack Abramoff.

390. Former Representative John Doolittle (R-CA) claimed to be an "ardent opponent of casino gambling," yet he was entangled with Jack Abramoff's fraudulent casino and lobby affairs. His wife's involvement in PAC was also suspect, as her company profited from his campaign contributions. His decision not to run for reelection was a wise one, considering how distracting his fight against the legal proceedings linking him to Abramoff were.

391. Doolittle also accepted $14,000 in campaign donations from Abramoff and a lot more from his clients.

392. Julie Doolittle, Rep. John Doolittle's wife, was paid about $30,000 for bookkeeping work for a nonprofit firm set up by the lobbying group Alexander Strategy Group. This firm was founded by Edwin Buckham, former chief of staff to Tom Delay. ASG set up the U.S. Korea-U.S. Exchange Council, which funded luxury trips abroad for members of Congress.

Fox News: "Fair and Balanced"?

393. FOX News openly supports the Republican Party, as evidenced by Rupert Murdoch's News Corp's $1 million donation to the Republican Governors Association in 2010, among other biases.

394. Nathan Daschle, executive director of the Democratic Governors Association, said of News Corp/Fox News's $1 million contribution to the GOP, "For a media company—particularly one whose slogan is 'fair and balanced'—to be injecting themselves into the outcome

of races is stunning. The people owning Fox News have made a decision that they want to see Democratic governors go down to defeat. It's a jaw-dropping violation of the boundary between the media and corporate realm."

395. News Corporation's donation to the Republican Governors Association in 2010 is one of the biggest ever given by a media organization, according to several campaign finance experts.

396. Media Matters for America, a liberal group that has tangled often with Rupert Murdoch's News Corp/Fox News, call the company plainly "an appendage of the Republican Party."

397. The Democratic National Committee said in an email to reporters that Fox News's famous slogan, "Fair and Balanced," is "rendered utterly meaningless." Democratic National Committee spokesman Hari Sevugan said that Fox News's political coverage "should have a disclaimer for what it truly is—partisan propaganda."

American Legislative Exchange Council and Koch Industries

398. Founded in 1973 by Paul Weyrich and other right-wing activists zealots, the American Legislative Exchange Council is an arm of the Republican network of policy shops that, with substantial infusions of corporate cash, has evolved to shape American politics.

399. Some of ALEC's goals for the 2011 session were to privatize education, break unions, deregulate major industries, and pass voter ID laws.

400. Koch Industries's top lobbyist was once ALEC's chairman. As a result, the Koch conglomerate has shaped legislation touching every state in the country. Like ideological venture capitalists, the Koch Brothers have used ALEC as a way to invest in radical right-wing ideas and fertilize them with millions of dollars.

401. Bob Edgar of Common Cause, a nonprofit, nonpartisan, political organization, said of ALEC, "Dozens of corporations are investing millions of dollars a year to write business-friendly legislation that is being made into law in statehouses coast to coast, with no regard for the public interest."

402. A prominent example of ALEC drafting model bills and handing them off to legislators is when George W. Bush signed into law—as one of his first actions as governor of Texas—an ALEC model bill that gives immunity to corporations if they tell regulators about their violations of environmental regulations. Lobbyists like Koch Industries would benefit from this limitation of environmental litigation.

Joe Barton and Big Oil

403. Senator Joe Barton (R-TX) has been named by Dirty Energy Money as one of Congress's "dirtiest politicians, with nearly $2 million in dirty energy money contributions since 1999, 57 percent of which come from oil companies."

404. Dirty Energy Money also found that Senator Barton "votes with Big Oil 100 percent of the time and has consistently voted against an end to oil and gas subsidies

and most recently for removing the EPA's authority to regulate greenhouse gases.

405. Chair of the House Energy and Commerce Committee from 2004–2006, Barton has received over $1 million from the energy industry, including $22,000 from Exxon Mobil in PAC contributions from 2000 to 2006.

406. Representative Joe Barton has been instrumental in postponing legislative action and disseminating misleading information on global warming. Barton chaired the Energy and Air Quality Subcommittee before serving as chair of the full committee. He is quoted as saying that the regulation of greenhouse gas emissions is "off the table indefinitely."

407. Senator Joe Barton (R-TX) apologized to BP CEO Tony Hayward for the $20 billion required of BP to clean up and compensate victims of BP's 4.9 million barrel oil spill in the Gulf of Mexico: "I'm ashamed of what happened in the White House yesterday. I think it is a tragedy of the first proportion that a private corporation can be subjected to what I would characterize as a shakedown, in this case, a $20 billion shakedown."

408. In response to Senator Barton's apology to BP for making them pay for the spill, Press Secretary Robert Gibbs said, "What is shameful is that Joe Barton seems to have more concern for big corporations that caused this disaster than the fishermen, small business owners and communities whose lives have been devastated by the destruction. Congressman Barton may think that a fund to compensate these Americans is a 'tragedy,' but most Americans know that the real tragedy is what the

men and women of the Gulf Coast are going through right now."

409. Oil and gas companies have contributed over $100,000 to Senator Barton since the beginning of 2009. He has received the second-highest amount of money from oil and gas companies out of all members of the House Energy and Commerce Committee.

410. Even members of Barton's own party called for Barton to resign from his position as the ranking Republican on the Energy and Commerce Committee after hearing of Barton's siding with BP after the oil spill. Rep. Jeff Miller, a Florida Republican, said, "Mr. Barton's remarks [apologizing to BP for being asked to fund the cleanup of the Gulf] are out of touch with this tragedy and I feel his comments call into question his judgment and ability to serve in a leadership on the Energy and Commerce Committee. He should step down as Ranking Member of the Committee."

411. After being reprimanded for his apology to BP, Joe Barton, when asked if he planned to remain the ranking Republican on the Energy and Commerce Committee, declared, "Damn straight."

James Inhofe and Big Oil

412. Senator James M. Inhofe (R-OK) described global warming as the "greatest hoax ever perpetrated on the American people."

413. Senator Inhofe has received $1,287,950 from the oil and coal industries since 1999 and "sided with Dirty

Energy interests in 100% of selected votes," according to Dirty Energy Money.

414. Senator Inhofe, ranking Republican on the Environment and Public Works Committee attempted to silence proponents of global warming by turning the debate into a "McCarthyite witch-hunt" to criminalize the activities of leading climatologists, as it was put by Rick Piltz, a former official in the U.S. government climate science program who now runs the Climate Science Watch website.

415. There was an increase in hate mail to climate scientists after emails from the Climatic Research Unit (CRU) at the University of East Anglia were hacked, stolen, and published online. Senator Inhofe is attributed with fueling these distracting emails.

416. On the list of seventeen climatologists targeted by Senator Inhofe is Michael Mann, the climatologist who created the "hockey stick" chart used by Al Gore to support global warming theories. Mann has received hate mail since Inhofe's campaign and says, "Some of the emails make thinly veiled threats of violence against me and even my family, and law enforcement authorities have been made aware of the matter."

Campaigns and Corporations

417. The top recipients of campaign contributions from the energy/natural resource industry are the following Republicans: Rick Perry (received $1,499,961), Mitt Romney ($1,562,092), David Dewhurst ($842,551), and John Boehner ($735,805).

418. "[Obama] raised more in sub-$200 contributions than each Republican candidate's overall total." Meanwhile, Romney "leads Republicans in raising larger contributions." While more than half of Obama's campaign fundraising comes in the lowest bracket (sub-$200, 53 percent of his total funds), it's telling that Romney is at the other end of the fundraising spectrum, with 58 percent of his total funds coming from the highest size-of-donation bracket ($2,500 maximum).

419. Mitt Romney's fundraising is both successful (over $75 million in March 2012) and mysterious. The names of Romney's major fundraisers (and "bundlers" who host parties and encourage others to contribute to Romney's campaign) are withheld, therefore keeping secret the information of which individuals and corporations support and might later benefit from Romney's campaign. Why all the secrecy? President Obama's campaign organization disclosed not only the identities of bundlers, but also their fundraising thresholds.

420. Of the $75 million raised by Romney's campaign, about $49 million was donated from donors who maxed out the legal limit of campaign donations ($2,500 each). Only $6.5 million came from supporters at the lowest end of the contribution spectrum ($200 or less). If Romney only cares about the wealthy while fundraising, you can bet he will favor them if elected.

421. Michael Malbin, director of the Campaign Finance Institute, noted that Romney's campaign relies heavily on "maxed-out" donors who have donated the legal limit for donations to a candidate's campaign: $2,500. Romney received 66 percent of his contributions from

these high-end donors, more than any other presidential candidate since 2003.

422. Michael Malbin also remarked, "Romney is less focused on small donors than any other candidate at this stage of the campaign in recent memory. And that is parallel to a larger problem: He has not yet excited the passions of the kind of people who give small contributions or volunteer their time."

423. An NPR analysis found that only 10 percent of Romney's contributions have come from people giving $200 or less. That is low compared to his fellow Republicans' small donor constituents and extremely low compared to those of Democrat candidates. If big spenders are backing him, he'll likely return the favor if elected.

424. Once Romney's donors max out the $2,500 limit, they redirect their contributions to the independently run super PAC known as Restore Our Future. Out of the 15 millionaires and billionaires who gave $1 million to the super PAC, seven have hosted fundraising events for Romney or joined his state finance committees. A few of these mega-donors and bundlers are hedge fund founders Paul Singer and John Paulson, Tiger Management head Julian Robertson, William Koch, Francis Rooney, and Frank VanderSloot.

425. Mitt Romney's fundraising foundation comes from Wall Street ties created during his time starting and directing the private equity firm Bain Capital. Many of these Wall Street friends are organizers for the Romney fundraising campaign.

426. Goldman Sachs is Romney's biggest contributor, with over $426,000 coming from managers or employees at the firm in 2011. John Whitehead, Goldman Sachs's former chairman, and other executives at the firm are listed by the Romney campaign as fundraising events leaders.

427. Muneer Satter led fundraising events for Romney in 2011 and was a co-chairman of Romney's national finance committee when he ran for president in 2008. Satter is a managing partner at Goldman Sachs, and he gave $195,000 to Romney's super PAC (when maxing out the $2,500 legal limit to donate directly to a candidate was not enough).

428. Besides Goldman Sachs (with $535,680 donated to Romney's campaign from employees and managers), major contributors to Romney's campaign include the investment bank JPMorgan Chase & Co. ($375,650), Morgan Stanley ($323,800), international Swiss-based bank Credit Suisse ($299,160), and Citigroup ($282,765). Compare these leading backers to those of Obama (Microsoft, Google, University of California, and Harvard).

429. Within a matter of weeks of JPMorgan executives hosting a series of fundraisers for the Romney campaign, the campaign received over $60,000 from JPMorgan employees.

430. The Texas tax and accounting firm Ryan (led by G. Brint Ryan, a supporter of Rick Perry) provided Rick Perry with his largest amount of cash. Ryan employees contributed a total of $158,000 to the Perry campaign.

431. The financial sector accounts for the biggest slice of the Romney funds pie. Andrea Saul, a Romney spokeswoman, claimed that this is a result of frustration over Obama's economic policy. But this frustration is represented by corporations in the form of money handed over to Romney's campaign, not by everyday citizens.

432. Open Secrets asserts that Republicans are the main recipient of the energy and natural resources industry's political contributions: "Led by the oil and gas industry, this sector regularly pumps the vast majority of its campaign contributions into Republican coffers ... this sector has remained rock-solid red."

433. According to Open Secrets, during the 2011–2012 election cycle, "$23,136,059 in donations from the energy/natural resource industry went to Republicans, while $6,679,082 went to Democrats."

434. The Bush administration knew of the Enron scandal before it broke. Former Enron chief Kenneth Lay was a leading financial backer of Bush during his presidential campaign, and he privately discussed energy regulations for corporations with Dick Cheney.

435. Republicans argue that any attempt to end the Bush tax cuts for the highest earners, while continuing them for others, represents class warfare, while the numbers show that continuing the 2001 and 2003 tax cuts for everyone would cost $4.5 trillion over ten years, while extending them only for individuals making less than $200,000 a year and married couples making less than $250,000 would cost $3.7 trillion.

436. The most conservative and Republican sympathizing Supreme Court "in decades," according to the *New York Times,* ruled in Citizens United vs the Federal Election Commission that unlimited spending by corporations to persuade the voting public was permissible and constitutional, expanding the right to free speech from American citizens to corporations and business unions.

437. When offered the opportunity to end federal subsidies, totaling over $2.4 billion annually, to the top five big oil companies, Senate Republicans decided to stick to paying off the corporations despite these corporations being tremendously lucrative already and the evidence that subsidies won't lower gas prices in any way or benefit the middle class at all.

438. While Republicans claim that corporate taxes are too high, the website of nonprofit, nonpartisan organization Common Dreams reports that "U.S. Office of Management (OMB) figures ... show a gradual drop over the years in Corporate Income Tax as a Share of GDP, from 4% in the 1960s to 2% in the 1990s to 1.3% in 2010. That's one-third of what it used to be."

439. Also according to Common Dreams: "Also coming from the OMB [U.S. Office of Management] is the percent of Total Tax Revenue derived from corporate taxes. The corporate share has dropped from about 20% in the 1960s to under 9% in 2010."

440. Common Dreams also points out that "in a U.S. Treasury report of global competitiveness, it is revealed that U.S. corporations paid only 13.4% of their profits in taxes between 2000 and 2005, compared to the OECD average of 16.1%. A similar PayUpNow.org analysis of

100 of the largest U.S. companies found that less than 10% of pre-tax profits in 2010 were paid in non-deferred U.S. federal income taxes."

441. Just a year after BP's infamous oil spill in the Gulf, Sarah Palin readjusted her schedule in order to hold a meeting with Tony Hayward, BP's chief executive, to try to persuade him to support her Alaska Gasline Inducement Act. He declined, believing it was a bad deal.

442. One of the controversial "video news release[s]" (VNRs) in 2006 under the Bush Administration was broadcast by Medialink Worldwide and titled, "Global Warming and Hurricanes: Hot Air?" The client of the segment was identified as "TCS Daily Science Roundtable," but it was not disclosed that TCS (Tech Central Station) was a project by the Republilcan lobbying and PR firm DCI group, of which ExxonMobile is a client. ExxonMobile also gave TCS $95,000 in 2003 for "climate change support." The VNR ridiculed claims that the increase in hurricane activity is related to global warming.

443. Super PACs have been the most dominant spenders in the 2012 Republican presidential primary, with men like hedge-fund manager John Paulson, the Marriott brothers, and casino magnate Sheldon Adelson funnelling millions into the PACs in support of the GOP and their tax cuts for the wealthy.

444. Minnesota House and Senate Republicans have moved forward on an initiative to cut state property taxes on businesses by reducing the tax refunds for 313,000 residents who earn less than $55,000 by $213 on average. The tax cut for business is estimated to eventually cost the state treasury $800 million.

445. South Carolina Republican lawmakers aim their portion of the $25 billion settlement brokered between the state and the nation's biggest banks on behalf of the homeowners to fund more corporate tax cuts and incentives.

446. National Republican Congressional Committee Chairman Congressman Pete Sessions received a preferential VIP loan unavailable to ordinary borrowers from defunct lender Countrywide Financial Corp., even though House ethics rules state that legislators can only receive "loans from banks and other financial institutions on terms generally available to the public." The VIP mortgage was issued in 2007 and was worth as much as $1 million. The loan did not appear on any of Sessions's annual financial disclosure reports.

447. Buck McKeon (R-CA) also received a special $315,000 loan from Countrywide in the late 1990s, as part of their VIP program.

448. Elton Gallegly (R-CA) also admitted to being told that the $77,000 loan he received from Countrywide Financial Corp.'s VIP program was preferential and below the market value.

449. Representative David Rivera (R-FL) lobbied for a contract between Flagler Dog Track and Millennium Marketing, a company co-owned by Rivera's mother. At first, Rivera denied working for the dog track, but later admitted to managing the campaign. About $500,000 were secretly handed over to the owners of Flagler Dog Track as a result of this contract.

450. When Newt Gingrich appeared on stage embracing the support of David Rivera, even his own party members

thought the Republican alliance was a bad move. Tom Slade, a former Republican Party chairman, said, "I saw Rivera standing behind him on that damn platform and I said to myself, '[Gingrich] can't be that stupid.'"

451. Additionally, Congressman Rivera lied about his source of income. He claimed that he was a consultant to U.S. Agency for International Development, but they reported that he was never hired.

452. While Stephen Fincher (R-TN) lent his campaign $250,000 free of interest, he reported no personal assets other than his farm, no bank accounts, stocks and no bonds. He also drives an expensive vehicle and pays tuition at a private school.

453. The STOCK Act, which would curb insider trading by lawmakers, underwent a removal of the significant provision where anyone trading on political intelligence would have to register like a lobbyist. The removal was headed by Majority Leader Rep. Eric Cantor (R-VA).

454. Rep. Charles Bass (R-NH) denied the substantial evidence that his sponsorship of legislation to encourage renewable energy systems took place because of meetings with his nephew, Steven Walker, president of New England Wood Pellet. Coincidentally, wood pellet systems were included as some of those renewable energy systems in the NEWP-supported legislation. By May 2010, Bass had a $1 million stake in NEWP.

CHAPTER SIX

THE WORKING MAN

There are a lot of people in this country who are unemployed. Many of these people try desperately to find a solid source of income to support themselves and their family. You also have many students graduating from college who have to find menial minimum-wage jobs or take unpaid internships.

The majority of Americans, however, are hard-working people, who work over forty hours a week, some even working more than one job to make ends meet. While these people are trying to pay their bills and stay financially afloat, most Republicans are on easy street, with the majority of them getting their millions from the 'family business' or from money being 'passed down.' Now we're not saying that none of them have earned their fortunes, but a large number of them have always been in the power elite, and while they did work, it's not like they started in the mail room.

It's hard for someone who's had a silver spoon in their mouth from a young age to understand the plight of the working man. They've never lived paycheck to paycheck or had to make choices between bills to pay.

With this said, it's no surprise that they don't go out of their way to make it easy for the middle class. The truth is, they don't understand the middle class…and going even further, they don't care to! All they care about is making their millions, getting bills passed that work in their favor, and making sure that their rich friends are happy. So when it comes to the everyday family who are trying to carry a mortgage, put their kids through college, and save some money for retirement (if their lucky), it would be nice if the government in which they pay so much in taxes to would look out for their best interest in making sure that they succeed.

Yeah, when pigs fly.

The middle class obviously means nothing to them, and they're not going to go out of their way for a group that doesn't plan on voting for them. But why should they? They're given no reason to. But what do the Republicans care, they know they're set for life, so why waste time and pay more taxes so that the middle class can live more comfortably?

455. Historically, when Republicans are in the White House, the economy shows less growth.

456. Conservapedia, the conservative version of Wikipedia, does not have an entry for the term "middle class."

457. Newt Gingrich had this dismissive message for the participants of the Occupy movement fighting for economic equality: "Go get a job right after you take a bath."

458. Republicans are quick to cut funds for governmental positions, which are often dominated by women.

459. Chairman of the House Budget Committee Rep. Paul Ryan (R-WI) refused to define the word "rich," since he believes that the wealthiest 1 percent of Americans are the "job creators." Yet again, Republicans show a marked reluctance to acknowledge income inequality.

460. Conservative think tank The Heritage Foundation unsurprisingly echoes the right-wing's inability to address the problem of uneven wealth distribution, claiming that economic inequality is simply a sign of prosperity.

461. Republicans have strayed from predecessors Abraham Lincoln (who said, "labor is the superior of capital, and deserves much the higher consideration") and Ronald Reagan (who said "collective bargaining...has played a major role in America's economic miracle. Unions represent some of the freest institutions in this land"). In the GOP presidential race in 2012, opposing collective bargaining is a popular policy among candidates.

462. Republican National Committee chairman Reince Priebus said in an NBC's *Today Show* interview in 2011 that Obama was responsible for the loss of "26 million jobs." However, this number is inflated by a factor of ten.

463. Newt Gingrich said, "One of the things the Congress should do immediately is defund the National Labor Relations Board."

464. A Mitt Romney ad aired in South Carolina stated, "The National Labor Relations Board [is] now stacked with union stooges selected by the president."

465. Rick Santorum said, "I do not believe that state, federal or local workers … should be involved in unions. "I would actually support a bill that says that we should not have public employee unions for the purposes of wages and benefits to be negotiated."

466. Wisconsin Governor Scott Walker (R) has been using John Mellencamp's song "Small Town" at reelection campaign events. This might not be an informed song choice, as Mellencamp is pro-union, and Governor Walker has come under fire recently for fighting collective bargaining. While Mellencamp hasn't demanded Walker stop using his song, he has reminded the public that he stands apart from Republicans, though they inexplicably continue to use his music during campaigns without acknowledging the sharp difference in the musician's political values.

467. Michigan Senate Minority Leader Gretchen Whitmer (D- East Lansing) said, "Michigan's working families need to make their voices heard and tell these Republicans that Right to Work simply means Right to Work for less. Republicans have already increased taxes on working families to pay for corporate tax cuts and it's time we end this attack on the middle class and stand up for Michigan's workforce."

468. Rick Perry supports erecting structural barriers that keep workers from organizing, saying that this would make Texas a powerful "magnet" to job creation.

469. Mitt Romney believes that legislation making it harder for unions to organize "makes a lot of sense."

470. In April 2012, House Speaker Bill O'Brien (R-NH) decided the consequences of opposition to his anti-labor Right to Work legislation would be to put a couple of dissenters farther away from the podium. Representative Toni Soltani, who openly opposed the Right to Work bill, is considering legal action over the fact that

despite Soltani's "limp and inability to walk quickly" that makes it difficult for him to get past obstacles when walking up to take parliamentary action, O'Brien has seated him in the back and shut down Soltani's requests and others' offers to switch seats.

471. House Speaker Bill O'Brien also sat Representative Tim Copeland, another opponent of Right to Work, at the back of the room in childish retaliation and attempts to fend off dissent. Said Representative Soltani, "Copeland had been initially assigned an aisle seat, but it was revoked "as a result of his votes and refusal to carry water for Speaker O'Brien." Copeland also explained, "Next thing I know I get a letter one day that said my seat assignment's been changed.... No other explanation ... It was just a form of retaliation from him."

472. Republican idol Ronald Reagan caused unemployment to rise to 10.8 percent as a result of his initial sharp tax cuts. Reagan subsequently raised taxes eleven times (which conservatives prefer to forget), and unemployment fell again while his approval ratings were restored.

473. A recent popular sentiment espoused by Republicans from Mitt Romney to Paul Ryan is that government needs to "broaden the tax base," which has come to represent Republicans' belief that poor people in America, working-class folk, do not pay enough taxes and rely too heavily on government social programs. The truth that the middle and lower class pay a share of the nation's total taxes roughly equivalent to its share of the nation's total income doesn't seem to hinder the Republicans' unfounded claim.

474. Kansas State Republicans aim to perform a complete overhaul on the tax code, by eliminating income taxes for residents and small businesses, lowering the sales tax and ditching a host of tax credits. The glaring problem with the plan is that all these changes omit anyone making less than $25,000 a year, an estimated half a million of the state's 2.9 million residents. In fact, taxes for the poor are estimated to be raised by $72 to account for the cuts.

475. Harrell Kirstein, press secretary for the New Hampshire Democratic Party: "Not only did Congressman Bass (R-NH) use his office to promote his nephew's company, and later made a lucrative investment in that company with nonpublic information, but now he is sponsoring a bill to make his own actions a crime. Those are the values of a lifelong member of Congress, not hard working New Hampshire citizens."

476. In an interview with *Manchester Union Leader,* Representative Frank Guinta (R-NH) denied receiving any loan to violate campaign personal finance laws. As for the quick appearance of a previously undisclosed bank account with $250,000 and $500,000 in assets, Guinta said that he only discloses his finances when his personal loans to his own campaigns come under scrutiny.

477. Governor Rick Scott (R-FL) had his economic team, headed by an array of CEOs (the list includes executives of companies like Blockbuster, Walt Disney Parks and Resorts, and Universal Orlando Resort), look into the issue of unemployment. The team used former Obama administration official Alan Krueger's research to underestimate the amount of time and effort the unemployed

use to look for work, and supported Scott's incorrect belief that they do not deserve government support because they are lazy. Krueger responded by saying that the team "misspelled my name and misused my study!"

478. Republicans have voted against raising the minimum wage every time it has come up in Congress.

479. In 2011, Republicans in Wisconsin voted to do away with the collective bargaining rights of state workers.

480. The Republican presidential hopefuls in 2012 have proposed tax cuts that would range from $6.6 trillion to $18 trillion over a decade with a large chunk of the cuts going to the the richest of Americans. Citizens for Tax Justice have estimated that the tax cuts received by the richest one percent would be on average 270 times the tax cuts received by the middle class.

481. In November 2011, a Congressional subcommittee charged with addressing the country's debt failed to reach agreement as Republicans offered to raise taxes by $300 billion over the next decade but retain tax protection for the most wealthy—leaving only the middle and lower classes in harm's way.

482. Congressional Republicans have tried to revive tax loopholes that would make foreign profits exempt from taxation to give businesses more incentive to go abroad and take middle class jobs with them.

483. Mitt Romney wants to eliminate the National Labor Relations Board. He said on the Howie Carr Show: "We gotta shut off the funding to this thing [the NLRB]. We

gotta shut it down .... I think cutting off funding and eliminating the NLRB ... may make more sense."

484. Mitt Romney has called union leaders, "union bosses who have no interest in a constructive relationship with management."

485. Romney offered his "110 percent" support to Ohio's anti-union Senate Bill 5, which would restrict collective bargaining rights for teachers, police officers, and firefighters in Ohio.

486. Mitt Romney claims that Obama is "out of touch" for working to create manufacturing jobs for young Americans. However, Joe Biden counters this statement by saying that "there is nothing out of touch about fighting for the future of the middle class by creating manufacturing jobs." While Romney was governor, manufacturing jobs declined by twice the national average in Massachussetts, but over 400,000 manufacturing jobs have been created under President Obama because of his tax incentives.

Republicans vs. Workers

487. Republicans touted their dedication to creating jobs during the 2010 campaign, but once they became the majority in the House of Representatives, the truth came out, as Senate Minority Leader Mitch McConnell (R-KY) admitted, that the "top political priority" of the GOP was to "deny President Obama a second term." They use the bait of job creation to get votes, but their main concern is smear campaigns, not the working class. Some of their proposals would even destroy jobs.

488. One way that Republicans shift focus from actively improving the job market is by working on distracting legislation about hot-button issues such as religious freedom, women's reproductive health, health care, the debt ceiling, gas prices ... the list goes on and on, but none of these measures actually creates jobs.

489. Because of a "single anonymous letter," Maine Gov. Paul LePage (R) ordered the removal of a thirty-six foot mural from the lobby of Maine's Department of Labor lobby. The letter claimed that the mural's depiction of Maine's labor history reminded him/her of "communist North Korea where they use these murals to brainwash the masses."

490. Also in Maine, acting labor chief Laura Boyett claimed that "some business owners" complained that they felt the mural in the Department of Labor lobby was hostile. LePage spokesman Dan Demeritt said that the mural, as well as the pro-labor names (like Cesar Chavez) of some Department of Labor conference rooms, were examples of "one-sided décor" that contradicted the labor department's pro-business values.

491. Wisconsin Governor Scott Walker's (R) law to dismantle collective bargaining rights has hurt civil servants such as nurses and teachers. At the same time, it helps prison inmates, who are getting the jobs that unionized workers used to hold.

492. Rick Santorum has told reporters, "Calling Rick Santorum a friend of labor is like calling Mitt Romney a conservative. Neither are true."

493. Wisconsin Governor Scott Walker (R) opposes collective bargaining, the same right sought by workers of the Triangle Shirtwaist Factory that was repeatedly refused before the infamous fire 101 years ago.

494. Richard Greenwald, author of *The Triangle Fire, the Protocols of Peace and Industrial Democracy in Progressive Era New York*, says that in the mid-twentieth-century, "unions were responsible for the formation of the middle class. By negotiating wages, benefits and hours, they made it possible for many workers to achieve membership in the middle class." Chris Christie, the governor of New Jersey (R), claimed the opposite: "The unions are trying to break the middle class in New Jersey."

495. Representative David Burns (R-Whiting, Maine) sponsored a bill in March 2011 to eliminate the maximum number of hours teens can work and create a $5.25 "training wage" for teenage workers that is under the state's minimum wage of $7.50 an hour. Before being enacted as a law, Burns's legislation underwent changes that removed the low wages; however, it did increase the number of hours that teens could work during school days to give kids longer hours and satisfy business owners hoping for more cheap labor.

496. The 99 percent versus the top 1 percent issue presented by Occupy Wall Street has its historical political reasoning to back it up, starting from the Reagan administration. The wealthiest Americans took no more than 12.8 percent of the total income between 1949 and 1979, and when Reagan took office,

the 1 percent controlled 10 percent of America's income. But this number spiked very rapidly starting from Reagan's last year as president, when the wealthiest 1 percent took 15.5 percent of the national income, up through George W. Bush's presidency, when that number shot up to 23.5 percent in 2007.

497. Republican policy is the biggest reason for the increase in the share of the top 1 percent, causing the distance between them and the rest of America. Paul Buchheit, a professor with City Colleges of Chicago and founder of fightingpoverty.org, asserts that "if middle- and upper middle-class families had maintained the same share of American productivity that they held in 1980, they would be making an average of $12,500 more per year ... [America's economy] has quintupled since 1980, and we all contributed to that success. But our contributions have earned us nothing. While total income has also quintupled, percentage-wise almost all the gains went to the richest 1 percent . . . . [This trend] translates into *a trillion extra dollars* of income every year for the richest 1 percent."

498. Joshua Holland, a senior writer at AlterNet and author of *The 15 Biggest Lies About the Economy: And Everything Else the Right Doesn't Want You to Know About Taxes, Jobs and Corporate America,* asserts that "those at the top of the ladder aren't any more virtuous, intelligent or hardworking than they were 30 years ago, and this didn't happen by accident. Some part of it may well have resulted from technological innovations, but the lion's share of that shift resulted from specific policy changes that the corporate Right fought hard to enact."

499. Joshua Holland also asserts that the increase in the 1 percent's share of America's wealth "resulted from the emergence of international trade deals that facilitated offshoring much of our manufacturing base, changes in labor laws and enforcement that cut the unionized share of the American workforce in half, and a shift in priorities at the Federal Reserve that led it to concentrate far more on keeping inflation in check than keeping working America employed." These were and are policies of Republican politicians.

500. "Interestingly, those at the top are no more likely to identify themselves as conservatives, or less likely to see themselves as liberals, than the other 99 percent. They aren't more likely to favor forced childbirth or worry about the War on Christmas—social issues— but they know where their bread is buttered (or buttered more heavily), so despite the fact that they don't differ much ideologically, they're significantly more likely to support Republicans."

501. Michele Bachmann and several other Republicans claim that extending unemployment benefits will incentivize Americans to remain unemployed and attack President Obama's attempts to do so.

502. The subprime mortgage crisis of the last decade that contributed to record breaking foreclosures throughout the country occurred under a Republican president, a Republican controlled Congress, and largely behind the fiscal ideology of former Republican (and Libertarian) Federal Reserve Chairman Alan Greenspan.

503. Despite evidence to the contrary—a large amount of statistical data pointing to two straight years of job growth and more than 3.9 million new private-sector jobs as of February 2012—the chair of the Republican National Committee, Reince Priebus, has recently said that "the situation is clearly not improving."

504. When a protester asked Mitt Romney what he would do to help the 99 percent, since he himself is part of the 1 percent, Romney responded that "those who try and divide the nation, as you're trying to do here and as our President is doing, are hurting this country… America's right and you're wrong."

505. Wisconsin Governor Republican Scott Walker signed a law that makes it more difficult for women to battle wage discrimination and challenge unfair compensation.

506. While Republicans continually put more money in the pockets of American millionaires, they are attempting to exclude many Americans from collecting unemployment on the grounds that they made too much money. For the record, Republicans think that those who made $100,000 or more annually are too rich to receive unemployment benefits, but those who made $1 million or more can not afford to pay higher taxes.

507. Governor Walker insisted that any indication of gender inequality in wages results from the fact that women put childrearing ahead of career goals and that "money is more important for men."

508. In 2008, Republicans nixed the Lilly Ledbetter Fair Pay Act signed by President Obama. The law would take

a big step toward gender equality by fighting unfair wages based on gender discrimination.

509. Rep. Tim Huelskamp (R-KS) called President Obama's acknowledgement of class differences "un-American." Apparently, Huelskamp would prefer to ignore Americans living in poverty, rather than recognizing disparity in American wealth distribution.

Middle Class Tax Policy

510. Tom Perriello, Former Democratic U.S. representative from Florida and president and CEO of the Center for American Progress Action Fund, writes in an article on CNN, "It's likely that a middle-class family with two kids making about $70,000 a year would pay about $1,150 more in income tax, according to calculations made by the Center for American Progress. That's an 80% increase over what they pay now, while million-aires will pay less."

511. The GOP budget proposed by House Budget Committee Chairman Paul Ryan would mean that the $5,500 the average middle-class family receives in federal support would be labeled as "nondefense discretionary spending" and cut by about 25 percent, or about $1,400 a year. These "nondefense" causes include education, health and science research, transportation, federal law enforcement, protection of natural resources, and consumer safety.

512. An unattributed *New York Times* editorial appearing in September 2010: "If Republicans are the least bit serious about reducing the deficit, they have to acknowledge

that doing so requires additional revenues, $700 billion of which would be lost to the top 2 percent of earners in the next decade if their taxes do not rise."

513. Steven Rattner, a contributing writer for *New York Times* Op-Ed and a longtime Wall Street executive, writes, "In 2010, 37 percent of these additional earnings went to just the top 0.01 percent, a teaspoon-size collection of about 15,000 households with average incomes of $23.8 million. These fortunate few saw their incomes rise by 21.5 percent."

514. The House Republican Budget eliminates Pell grants for students who are enrolled in classes less than half-time—over 1 million students over the next ten years—often lower-income students who are forced to work while in school.

515. Ron Paul supports a low flat tax, even though he has characterized it as "punishing to the poor and middle class."

516. Republican demands to cut federal programs resulted in the loss of an estimated 370,000 jobs in 2011.

517. House Budget Committee Chairman Paul Ryan's proposed Budget creates tax incentives for American businesses to send jobs overseas. Outsourcing not only means that job opportunities are being moved out of America, but also that more of the tax burden is left to the middle class.

518. The Republican party's primary concern is keeping the rich wealthy.

519. Despite the clear economic alliance of the Republican Party with America's wealthiest citizens, Republican campaigns rely on, as Daniel Dickey puts it, "involvement of strongly divided issues like abortion, gay marriage, immigration, defense spending, etc. What they have done is used ideologies to win over a larger audience. They swept their true motives under a carpet of religious values and American nationalism."

520. David Holtz of Progress Michigan states that the Republican party is "ideologically driven and corporate owned." Their campaign money comes from corporate support, so it is in a Republican candidate's best interests to side with wealthy corporations, rather than middle-class Americans.

521. Labor journalist Sam Pizzigati at The Institute for Policy Studies wrote in an article at Roots Action that, contrary to Republican interests, "if the federal government started taxing the wealthy and their corporations at the same rates in effect a half-century ago, the federal debt to investors would almost totally disappear over the next decade."

522. Labor journalist Sam Pizzigati at The Institute for Policy Studies also wrote in an article at Roots Action that, again, contrary to Republican interests, "After taxes, and after adjusting for inflation, 2008's top 400 had a staggering $38.5 billion more left in their pockets than 1955's most awesomely affluent. Multiply that near $40 billion by the annual tax savings the rest of America's richest 1 percent have enjoyed over recent years and you have an enormous war chest for waging class war,

billions upon billions of dollars available for bankroll-ing think tanks and candidates and right-wing media."

523. While Mitt Romney argues that concern for the poor is unfounded because they rely on safety nets, labor journalist Sam Pizzigati writes in an article at Roots Action that while Romney expresses concern for the middle class, he "doesn't seem to realize how much of the middle class is becoming poor." Pizzigati also says that, "According to an analysis of census data by the Center for Labor Market Studies at North-eastern University, 37 percent of young families with children were in poverty in 2010. It's likely that rate has worsened."

524. Democrats.org reports: "While he rips apart the social safety net that middle-class and low-income Ameri-cans rely on, [Rep. Paul] Ryan's budget extends all of the Bush tax cuts for the wealthiest Americans, providing $3 trillion more in tax cuts for the rich and corporations—without specifying how we'd pay for them." We can only assume that the 99 percent would foot the bill.

525. Steven Rattner, a contributing writer for *New York Times* Op-Ed and a longtime Wall Street executive, writes, "Government has also played a role [in the increasing disparity between the wealthy and the rest of the nation], particularly the George W. Bush tax cuts, which, among other things, gave the wealthy a 15 percent tax on capital gains and dividends. That's the provision that caused Warren E. Buffett's secretary to have a higher tax rate than he does."

526. Tim Dickinson at *Rolling Stone* wrote in November 2011, "Republicans have responded to the worst economic crisis since the Great Depression by slashing inheritance taxes, extending the Bush tax cuts for millionaires and billionaires, and endorsing a tax amnesty for big corporations that have hidden billions in profits in offshore tax havens. They also wrecked the nation's credit rating by rejecting a debt-ceiling deal that would have slashed future deficits by $4 trillion— simply because one-quarter of the money would have come from closing tax loopholes on the rich."

527. House Minority Leader Nancy Pelosi (D-CA) used a weekly news conference in December 2011 to compare the tax plans of the GOP and President Obama. For one thing, Pelosi said that the GOP plan "pays for the payroll-tax cut by eliminating 200,000 jobs."

528. In 2011, New Jersey Governor Chris Christie (R) hurt middle class families by cutting the Earned Income Tax Credit and homestead rebates, while at the same time finding money in the budget for corporate tax cuts.

529. According to Democrats, Rep. Paul Ryan's budget goes against last year's bipartisan agreement to reduce the deficit.

530. The GOP budget plan ensures continued defense expenditures by undoing the $55 billion cut scheduled for the Pentagon budget.

531. Dan Pfeiffer, the White House Communications Director, said that the Republican budget plan "fails the test of

balance, fairness, and shared responsibility" and "draws on the same wrong-headed theory that led to the worst recession of our lifetimes and contributed to the erosion of middle-class security over the last decade."

532. The Republican budget caps domestic discretionary spending—including funds to be used for programs like Medicaid, Social Security, and Medicare—at $1.028 trillion, which is $20 billion less than what was agreed to by both parties last year.

533. In yet another example of religion's inappropriate influence on the Republican Party's ability to govern, Rep. Louie Gohmert (R-TX) finds support for his tax policy in the Bible, stating, "I've pointed out before Jesus never said, 'Go ye therefore, use and abuse your taxing authority, take somebody else's money to help.' He said you do it with your own money and the best example is what Zacchaeus did after he met Jesus. He went and cut taxes."

Chapter Seven

Government Spending, Taxes, and Budgets

It's obvious when listening to a Republican speak that they are usually not talking from experience. When they want to cut the budget for teachers, police officers, or fire fighters, we know that they've never held these important positions, so do not fully understand the importance of them. They'll yell that the fire fighters have a lower response time, but they're the ones who closed the fire houses. They'll scream that students are failing, but they're not letting teachers use updated textbooks.

These people think that just because they're in a high position in government, they have all the answers. As we can plainly see, that is certainly not the case. They feel that they know better than the people who do it for a living, and that there are more important places for that money to go . . . where, to the war?

In addition to this, these very same teachers, police officers, and fire fighters are paying more in taxes than anyone else in the country. How does it make sense that the people who make the most money in this country pay the least amount of taxes, while the middle class pays the most? It doesn't! People from all over the world come to this country to try and prosper . . . but if the Republicans get their way, then the only people prospering will be them, and everyone else will drown. Surprisingly, they don't seem to care.

Two definitions of democracy are:

- Control of an organization or group by the majority of its members.
- The practice or principles of social equality.

From what we can see, the majority of the members most certainly do not have control, and there is definitely no social equality. The rich reign supreme, and everyone else can either deal with it or leave. This is not what the founding fathers had in mind ... not by a long shot.

534. Stephen Moore, founder of the Club for Growth (an outside group with Wall Street ties that often pressures more moderate Republican politicians to change their policies), said, "We're trying to let [2012] candidates know that if they ever voted for a tax increase, we'll never support them and in fact we'll work to defeat them. We're trying to get the word out to even the lowest grass-roots level that if you're a Republican you aren't allowed to vote for taxes."

535. Many Republicans today point to Reagan as an example of the ideal conservative president who set the precedent for serious tax cuts. But historian Douglas Brinkley, the editor of Reagan's diaries, points out that this is a "false mythology" of Reagan. The difference is that though Reagan made sharp cuts in taxes in his first year in office, he did not decrease spending to match it, and so he raised taxes eleven times during his administration, a fact conservatives ignore.

536. Ronald Reagan nearly tripled the federal budget deficit during his presidency, a fact that conservatives today ignore when they point to Reagan as an example of sound tax-cutting policy.

537. Alan Brinkley, a historian of the Depression, said of President Obama's activity in May 2010: "This is not the New Deal, but it's a significant series of achievements. And given the difficulty of getting anything done under the [Republicans'] gridlock of Congress, it's pretty surprising."

538. States that lean towards the Republican Party, at least in the 2004 presidential election, generally receive more in federal dollars than they pay in taxes.

539. Regarding 2012 state spending budgets, Senate Democrats argue that although government spending needs to be cut, "Republicans' reckless spending plan would cost jobs and make communities less safe."

540. Former chairman of the Minnesota Republican Party Tony Sutton, through reckless spending, awarding contracts worth hundreds of thousands of dollars to consultants, lawmakers, candidates, and party insiders, has left the group $2 million in debt before his resignation in January 2012.

541. Missouri House Republicans have proposed a budget for 2013 that is $1 billion more than the budget proposed by Governor Jay Nixon, a Democrat, but at the same time cuts $28.7 million from a program for the blind.

542. The Republican budget proposed for 2013 is fiscally irresponsible in that it offers a deficit of $833 billion for

the 2013 fiscal year, which precedent dictates will be significantly higher.

543. A large amount of the figures in the House budget proposed by Republicans regard budget outlays, budget deficits, and fiscal years in the far future—2030 to 2050. These numbers are largely meaningless and tend to be deceptively inaccurate.

544. Policy advisor Laurence M. Vance argues that the Republicans' House budget focuses on military and strategic cuts to social programs and education that will reinforce the United States position as both a welfare and warfare state.

545. In 2012, Republicans in Massachusetts have proposed a cap on state spending that Democrats argue would limit that state's ability to help vulnerable residents or communities hit by natural disasters, like the brush fires that wracked Monson, Brimfield, and Springfield months before the GOP proposal.

546. Republican Congressman Stephen Fincher's campaign involved supporting cuts in government spending, while he received millions in federal farm subsidies. Dr. Ron Kirkland campaign manager Brent Leatherwood said in an August 1 statement: "Mr. Fincher presents himself as the humble 37-year-old farmer who only makes $50,000 to $75,000 a year. However, Crockett County property records show he lives in a home valued near $250,000, drives an expensive SUV, uses state-of-the-art farm equipment and pays tuition at one of Jackson's finest private schools. How does he have the resources to drop $250,000 into this race? These numbers only add up in Washington."

547. Representative Gary Miller (R-CA), one of the wealthiest members of Congress, often asked his aides to handle his personal and business affairs, including looking for concert tickets and sending flowers to his family members and friends. This is an illegal use of a congressmember's staff.

548. In 2011, House Republicans voted to slash food assistance for low-income families at the same time they voted to approve funding for the upkeep of azaleas at the National Arboretum. In essence, Republicans think that flowers are worth government money, but American families are not.

549. Republicans defend the 2013 GOP budget as a way to decrease the deficit. However, deficit reduction would only be achieved through the dramatic cuts to social programs—like Medicare and Medicaid—that benefit millions of Americans. Republicans would rather leave low-income and elderly citizens without assistance that come up with a comprehensive bipartisan budget plan.

550. A study by Citizens for Tax Justice showed that Republican policy allowed thirty corporations with profits of $160 billion to not only get out of paying income tax, but to receive tax refunds during the period of 2008 to 2010.

551. The 2013 Republican budget slashes funding for research and development, thereby impeding progress and stunting American innovation.

552. Rep. Paul Ryan's 2013 budget neglects the needs of infrastructure. Deep cuts to transportation spending will not only negatively impact all Americans by lowering

the quality of public roads and transportation services, but will also result in many lost jobs.

553. In 2006, even the Bush Administration Treasury was forced to admit that extending the Bush tax cuts would have no real long-term beneficial effect on the economy.

554. No nonpartisan economists agree with the Republican idea that tax cuts pay for themselves and stimulate the economy.

555. The Congressional Budget Office has reported it is possible to dramatically improve the deficit outlook with a single legislative measure—ending Bush tax cuts. If Congress simply stopped passing the tax cuts of which the GOP is so fond, the deficit situation would steadily improve over the next decade.

556. In 2010, Senate Republicans voted to block the extension of tax cuts for 98 percent of Americans.

557. Republican taxation policy hurts children. Research shows that states with higher taxes—states that can invest more in libraries, schools, social programs, and community outreach—show better health and quality of life for children. The GOP plan to cut taxes across the board has a demonstrated detrimental effect on child welfare.

558. A study by Citizens for Tax Justice and the Institute on Taxation and Economic Policy have found that as a result of GOP policy, GE's tax rate over the past decade is 2.3 percent of its $81 billion in profits.

559. Under President Bush, Republican congressmen John Boehner, Eric Cantor, and Paul Ryan voted for tax cuts

for the wealthy, numerous wars, and high cost prescription drugs and never paid for them. Now congressmen Boehner, Cantor, and Ryan want to pay for tax cuts for the wealthy, numerous wars, and high cost prescription drugs with largely ineffectual spending cuts that target the middle class.

560. Lobbyist and a conservative activist Grover Norquist has significantly influenced the GOP party's tax policy and has gotten virtually every Republican congressmen to sign a pledge to never even consider raising taxes and insist on raising revenue by way of spending cuts without compromise.

State Budgets

561. In 2011, Florida Governor Rick Scott (R) announced to his supporters that his budget would make Florida the most "fiscally conservative" in the nation. The budget intended to slash corporate income and property taxes, lay off 6,700 state employees, cut education funding by $4.8 billion, and cut Medicaid by almost $4 billion.

562. Governor John Kasich of Ohio (R) proposed cutting 25 percent of schools' budgets, $1 million from food banks, $12 million from children's hospitals, and $15.9 million from an adoption program for children with special needs in 2011.

563. Governor Tom Branstad (R) of Iowa began 2011 by proposing a budget that included a $200 million tax cut on commercial property taxes and corporate income but would cease spending on education, cut $42 million to state universities and fire hundreds of state workers.

564. Pennsylvania Governor Tom Corbett's (R) 2011 budget proposal intended to cut taxes for corporations, while freezing the salaries of educators, cutting dental coverage for Medicaid recipients, and eliminating more than half of the state's universities.

565. Tea Party Gov. Paul LePage of Maine intended to cut income taxes for Maine's wealthiest 1 percent, while actually raising property taxes for the state's middle class, with his 2011 budget proposal. After advocating "shared sacrifice," his so-called "jobs budget" aimed to strip health care funding from working parents, cut funding for education and infrastructure and raise the retirement age for state employees. LePage was still able to provide more than $200 million in tax cuts for large estates, big businesses and the super wealthy.

566. In 2011, Gov. Scott Walker (R-WI) planned to raise taxes on the poor, eliminate $26 million in tax credits for seniors and single mothers, and cancel property tax rebates for low-income citizens making less than $24,000 a year, all to remedy the misguided tax cuts he provided the rich earlier in the year.

567. Also in 2011, Governor Scott Walker and his extremely austere "Wisconsin Budget Repair Bill" removed collective bargaining rights from state labor unions, inciting protest, a legislative walkout, school closings, and eventually a recall election for Gov. Walker in 2012.

568. In South Carolina, Gov. Nikki Haley (R) has aims to end the state's corporate income tax, even while she calls for cutting physical education, K-12 schools, and Medicaid.

569. While facing a $493 million budget deficit in Kansas in 2011, Gov. Sam Brownback (R) has called for eliminating the corporate income tax while proposing a $50 million cut to education.

570. Also in Kansas, with majorities in both Houses, Republicans have proposed a cut to the federal Earned Income Tax Credit and push an estimated 6,500 families below the poverty line

571. In October 2010, Arizona Gov. Jan Brewer (R) severely cut the state's Medicaid program, leading to two deaths and leaving ninety-eight Arizonians waiting for transplant funding. After months of protests, Gov. Brewer eventually agreed to set aside $151 million for "life-saving" procedures, including transplants. However, House Republicans refused to restore funding for organ transplants because, as House Appropriations Committee chair Jon Kavanagh (R) said, "Not enough lives would be saved to warrant restoring millions in budget cuts."

572. Later, while peoples' lives were in danger due to these health care cuts, Governor Brewer signed tax cuts for businesses that total an estimated $538 million out of the state's coffers.

2012 Republican Budget

573. In 2012, House Budget Committee Chairman Paul Ryan proposed a budget that cuts Social Security benefits for most recipients.

574. House Republicans aim to move toward privatization of Medicare and raising premium costs for many seniors with their 2012 budget.

575. The recent House Republican budget plan slashes $871 billion from government investments in education, job training, scientific research, and transportation infrastructure over the next decade.

576. Republicans wish to enact large cuts to the Pell Grant program, limited access to higher education for low-income and middle-class students.

577. Speaker of the House John Boehner called the 2012 Republican budget proposal—which would provide the wealthiest Americans with the lowest tax rate since the Hoover administration; cut the Supplemental Nutrition Assistance Program (SNAP) that feeds those Americans who would otherwise go hungry; begin the process of eliminating Medicare with cuts and increasing premium costs; among other things—"a real vision of what we [Republicans] were to do if we get more control here in this town. It's still a Democrat-run town."

578. Howard Gleckman of the nonpartisan Tax Policy Center reveals that the 2012 Republican budget proposed by Chairman Paul Ryan would require closing tax loopholes to yield an extra $700 billion in revenue yearly. The problem is that no tax loopholes are suggested to be closed, Ryan even adamantly defends the major loopholes that directly benefit the wealthy, such as the ultra-low rates on income from capital.

579. "I am weary of mystery meat. The latest serving was dished out today by House Budget Committee Chairman Paul Ryan (R-WI), who released a fiscal plan that airily promises both trillions of dollars in tax cuts and a nearly balanced budget within a

decade, but never says how he'd get there," says Howard Gleckman.

580. More recently, in March 2012, House Budget Committee Chairman Paul Ryan has given the impression that he's perfectly willing to once again utilize the threat of government shutdown to push the Republican budget and agenda.

581. Tax Policy Center's Howard Gleckman claims that "[Paul] Ryan isn't saying that his budget implies cuts of $4.6 trillion in popular tax deductions, credits, and exclusions over 10 years, according to new estimates by the Tax Policy Center. And that ignores the $5.4 trillion in revenue lost from permanently extending the 2001/2003 tax cuts."

582. The budget House Budget Committee Chairman Paul Ryan presented for 2012, is "essentially, an effort to have low- and middle-class households bear the entire burden of closing the fiscal gap and bear the costs of financing an additional tax cut for high income households," according to Gleckman.

583. These 2012 Republican budget proposal would cost about $3.2 trillion over ten years, on top of the $0.3 trillion lost from repealing taxes enacted to pay for Affordable Care Act, the $1.1 trillion lost from the Republicans' desired reduction in the corporate tax rate, and the $5.4 trillion lost from first extending the Bush-Obama tax cuts. By 2022, simulation research shows, the tax policies Republican House Budget Chairman Ryan has specified would lower federal revenues to just 15.8 percent of GDP.

584. Paul Ryan is in essence gaming the system with his budget proposal, not asking the Congressional Budget Office to determine whether the proposal actually achieves its stated goals but rather asking the CBO to determine the effect of the budget assuming it achieves the goals stated within, making his proposal appear in a more favorable light.

585. The Republican House failed to pass the NOAA 2013 budget, which would have no cost no taxpayer dollars and would support scientifically sound climate research.

586. The Republican House 2013 budget requires the elimination of $4.6 trillion in tax breaks, but so far they have not indicated any plans to eliminate tax cuts. This is yet another indication that this budget is poorly planned.

587. Studies have shown that Rep. Paul Ryan's proposed budget would disproportionately hurt women.

588. The Ryan Budget chooses finance over families. The sole focus of the proposed budget for 2013 is cutting the deficit, without consideration for the welfare of the American public.

589. While Rep. Ryan's proposed budget professes to be doing everything possible to cut spending, it fails to put an end to Bush tax cuts, which were supposed to be temporary to begin with.

590. The nonpartisan Congressional Budget Office's analysis of the GOP budget suggests that it will actually increase the deficit.

591. The GOP budget would actually slow job growth. The required spending cuts would necessitate over 3 million lost jobs between 2013 and 2014.

Presidential Candidate Budget Proposals

592. Year 2012 Republican Presidential candidate Rick Santorum's suggested budget aims to reduce the corporate income tax rate from 35 percent to 17.5 percent—and to zero for manufacturers.

593. As President, Santorum intends to permanently repeal the 0.9 percent tax on wages and the 3.8 percent tax on investment income of high-income individual taxpayers that were imposed by the 2010 health reform legislation and are scheduled to take effect in 2013.

594. Massachusetts governor and presidential candidate Mitt Romney intends to allow tax provisions in the 2009 stimulus act and subsequently extended through 2012 to expire—notably including the American Opportunity tax credit for higher education, the expanded refundability of the child credit, and the expansion of the earned income tax credit (EITC).

595. Romney, like Santorum, would also permanently repeal the 0.9 percent tax on wages and the 3.8 percent tax on investment income of high-income individual taxpayers that were imposed by the 2010 health reform legislation and are scheduled to take effect in 2013.

596. Romney's tax plan would allow high-income households to pay about the same share of taxes as they

would if he extended the Bush tax cuts, but without the unidentified revenue increases, they would pay a considerably lower share.

597) Romney would cut taxes for nearly all households making between $50,000 and $75,000 but by far less than those with higher incomes. On average, those making $1 million or more would see their after-tax incomes rise by nearly 12 percent while incomes of households earning $50,000–$75,000 would rise by only about 2 percent.

598. Massachusetts Governor and presidential hopeful Mitt Romney has been often criticized for, among other things, providing vague and somewhat conflicting information as to where the money would come from to finance his cuts and other tax reductions.

599. Former Speaker of the House and Republican Presidential candidate Newt Gingrich proposes an individual "flat tax" that would create an optional alternative tax system with a single 15 percent tax rate, with three major modifications: 1) capital gains, dividends, and interest income would not be taxable; 2) taxpayers could claim a standard exemption of $12,000 for each individual and dependent; and 3) the plan would eliminate the standard deduction and most itemized deductions and credits but would retain deductions for mortgage interest and charitable contributions as well as the child and earned income tax credits.

600. As President, Gingrich would also permanently repeal the federal estate tax and the surtaxes contained

in the 2010 Patient Protection and Affordable Care Act (PPACA).

601. Texas Governor Rick Perry's tax plan would make four major changes: 1) reduce the corporate income tax rate from 35 to 20 percent; 2) allow for immediate expensing of all investment purchases; 3) fully exempt foreign-source income of U.S.-based corporations; and 4) eliminate all other tax expenditures not related to depreciation, R&D, or foreign-source income, ostensibly only concerned with assisting corporations and the very wealthy.

602. Perry intends to also permanently repeal the federal estate tax and the surtaxes contained in the 2010 Patient Protection and Affordable Care Act (PPACA).

General Taxation

603. The wealthiest 1 percent of Americans pay about half the rate they did in 1980, largely because of tax cuts for the wealthy enacted by Bush and other Republican politicians.

604. Republicans have tried to assert that the 3.8 percent federal health care tax would apply to all home sales, when in fact that is incorrect and the tax only applies to capital gains, couples with adjusted gross income of $250,000, and those who make more than $500,000 profit from the sale of their home. About 95 percent of households will not be affected.

605. Unlike President Obama, many Republicans wish exempt offshore earnings from U.S. tax liability.

606. *New York Times* columnist Bob Herbert writes, "The question that I would like answered is why anyone listens to this crowd anymore. G.O.P. policies have been an absolute backbreaker for the middle class. (Forget the poor. Nobody talks about them anymore, not even the Democrats.) The G.O.P. has successfully engineered a wholesale redistribution of wealth to those already at the top of the income ladder and then, in a remarkable display of chutzpah, dared anyone to talk about class warfare."

607. Phillip Slater writes for the *Huffington Post*, "Republicans, who have always hated democracy, wanted to create the caste system that exists in the most wretched Third World nations—a system in which a tiny minority of wealthy individuals live off the labor of the deeply impoverished 98%, and maintain their stranglehold through a corrupt military dictatorship."

608. In Michigan, Governor Rick Snyder (R) revised the state's already regressive budget to decrease business taxes by 83 percent ($1.6 billion) and increase individual income taxes by 23 percent ($1.4 billion). Snyder's plan is intended to create a better business environment that will be more conducive to job creation, but the Center on Budget Policy and Priorities has found that these corporate tax cuts have a low chance of creating jobs or improving a state's economy, and they often end up creating more hardships for lower-income households that received state and local services that are cut in these plans.

609. In Georgia, House Majority Leader Larry O'Neal (R) introduced a bill that would cut corporate taxes

by 33 percent and implement a flax income tax rate. Meanwhile, an austerity budget was passed by the Georgia House in 2011 that causes state university funding to be cut by $75 million and health insurance premiums increase by over 20 percent for employees of the state, teachers, and retirees. The income tax would also be raised on household necessities.

610. While GOP politicians are busy trying to cut taxes, many corporations are already skilled at avoiding taxes. A study conducted by Citizens for Tax Justice evaluated 265 corporations and found that they paid an average of 3 percent in state taxes, while the average state tax rate is over twice that amount (6.2 percent).

611. The Ryan plan increases the budget for defense to $554 billion in 2013 while cutting $261 from social safety net programs like food stamps, federal workers, and health care.

612. Joel Prakken, chairman of Macroeconomic Advisers, credited the GOP budget plan as "reasonable" but without measurable predicted outcomes. Prakken also said that GOP plans "would have little immediate effect relative to a plan [like President Obama's] that stimulates aggregate demand."

CHAPTER EIGHT

SOCIAL AGENDA

If you hear the Republican candidates today, you'll notice that, while they may be taking a stand against something, there's usually a back story that goes along with it. The social agenda of each candidate reflects highly on the decisions they make, what they stand for, and how they want to be perceived. We mentioned earlier about the separation of church and state, but when you listen to the Republicans, you'll see very quickly that they do not agree with that.

While a candidate may be in favor or a specific topic; whether taxes, rights, etc., we're seeing more and more that religion is something that they all care highly for. Now, could this be that a large number of red states are on the Bible belt? Possibly. But it could also be that they have such a strong sense of religion, which they want to force it down every single person's throat.

Now the topics of abortion and gay marriage are ones that people have strong opinions. Whatever your reasons are, I'm sure that they are valid to you, and we are not here to say that you are wrong. The whole basis of this country was to be founded on a place where people could have their own views and opinions, and not fear persecution for them.

If you've noticed, there are a lot of different races, religions, and opinions that people have in this country. But the main argument that has been made against gay marriage is that the Bible states that marriage is between a man and a woman. But what if you don't believe in the Bible—rather, what if the Bible isn't your religion's holy book? What if the Hebrew Bible or Torah is? What about the Qur'an? The point we're trying to make is that while it may be against someone's religion for people of the same sex to marry, it's not against everyone's. The idea of making a law based on a group's religion goes against the nation's motto of "freedom of religion." You cannot have freedom of religion if a law is enacted that is based on one particular faith. If two Jewish men want to get married, they are not allowed to because of Christian beliefs? Two women who are Atheists cannot get married for the same reason? It is just hypocritical to say that everyone has the freedom to practice and follow their own religion, but have to follow the rules set by a specific one.

And when it comes to abortion, it comes off as if most of those in favor of pro-life are anti-women. You cannot tell a woman that she is equal to a man, but then follow it up by telling her what she can and cannot do with her own body. Now, we understand that people are against the killing of innocent babies (or fetuses) that don't have the choice of living or dying, but if you've noticed, there have been more and more stories of doctors who regularly perform abortions being murdered. Wait, so these people are against the killing of an unborn fetus, but have no problem killing a doctor, who may be married with children?

Without us getting off on a tangent, you will see that Republicans all have a specific social agenda, and use it to their advantage. A lot of voters care about how Christian a candidate is, or what their religious stance is on gay marriage, more than they do about the way the candidate plans on improving our economy … and rather than the Republicans taking the high road, they feed right into it and start preaching from day one.

613. Although the Republican Party professes to champion small government, it seems to have no problem legislating its way into the personal lives of every American. Limiting who citizens can marry and what they can do in the event of pregnancy seems more like dictatorship than small government.

614. Even Ronald Reagan, the perennial darling of the GOP, opposed the Civil Rights Act and the Voting Rights Act.

615. A comprehensive review of the voting records and statements of GOP incumbents and candidates reveals that there are at least 111 Republicans who support shutting down the Department of Education.

616. In the past few years, Republicans have called for laws forbidding child labor, laws guaranteeing minimum wage, and laws protecting the environment to be wiped off the books. They've advocated cutting federal funding for organizations like the Public Broadcasting System, Head Start, which provides educational opportunity to poor children, and Planned Parenthood, which uses 97 percent of its funds to provide general, obstetrical and gynecological medical care to women, many of whom are rural and poor.

617. Some "Republicans are trying to block the reauthorization of the Violence Against Women Act ... which first passed in 1994 and has been reauthorized twice since then, increased federal penalties for domestic violence and provided funding for groups and services that aid victims of domestic abuse."

618. According to Melanie Roussell, DNC National Press Secretary, "[Rep.Paul] Ryan and the GOP seem to think

that we're investing too much in things like education, research and development, and rebuilding our nation's roads and bridges. [Ryan's budget] would slash investments in education by 45 percent and infrastructure by 24 percent. Their arbitrary cuts don't distinguish between the wasteful spending we need to eliminate and the investments we need to secure a strong future."

619. According to author Chris Mooney, "Many conservatives—especially on the Christian Right—believe the United States was founded as a "Christian Nation." They consider the separation of church and state a "myth," not at all assured by the First Amendment. And they twist history in myriad other ways, large and small, including Michele Bachmann's claim that the Founding Fathers "worked tirelessly" to put an end to slavery."

620. Says Stephen Moore, founder of the Club for Growth (an outside group with Wall Street ties that often pressures more moderate Republican politicians to change their policies), "I can say this because I'm not an elected official: the most selfish group in America today is senior citizens. Their demands on Washington are: 'Give us more and more and more.' They have become the new welfare state, and given the size and political clout of this constituency, it's very dangerous. One of the biggest myths in politics today is this idea that grandparents care about their grandkids. What they really care about is that that Social Security check and those Medicare payments are made on a timely basis."

621. Rick Santorum, while spseaking to students and faculty at Ave Maria University in 2008 about Satan's influence on America, said: "You say, 'What could be

the impact of academia falling?' Well, I would have the argument that the other structures that I'm going to talk about here had root of their destruction because of academia. Because what academia does is educate the elites in our society, educates the leaders in our society, particularly at the college level. And they were the first to fall."

622. Rick Santorum, while speaking to students and faculty at Ave Maria University in 2008 about Satan's influence on America, noted examples of "the corruption of culture, the corruption of manners, the corruption of decency is now on display whether it's the NBA or whether it's a rock concert or whether it's on a movie set."

623. Oklahoma state legislator Republican Sally Kern received sharp media backlash after her outlandish rant against the gay community, in which she compared homosexuality to "toe cancer" and said "it's the biggest threat our nation has, even more so than terrorism or Islam."

624. In its first five years, beginning in 2005, the Roberts-led Supreme Court issued conservative decisions 58 percent of the time. And in the term ending in 2009, the rate rose to 65 percent, the highest in any year since at least 1953.

625. Four of the six most conservative justices in American history (of the forty-four judges in total who have sat at the Supreme Court since 1937) are serving currently.

626. The Defense of Marriage Act, which effectively prohibited same sex marriages and limited the rights of all same sex couples, was introduced to the House by Republican Robert L. Barr, Jr. and became effective in

1996. Although voted into law by both Republicans and Democrats and signed by President Clinton, progressives, including President Obama, have maintained a platform of repeal, while Republicans, such as President George W. Bush, have claimed that the Act doesn't do enough to protect the conservative definition of marriage, and have even suggested constitutional amendments.

627. "Latinos are Republican. They just don't know it yet," said former President Ronald Reagan.

628. Republicans in Congress blocked the passage of a bill that would have given aid and extended benefits to homeless veterans and their children.

629. In a confusing and unsuccessful attempt to explain how the death penalty is pro-life, Senator Orrin Hatch has argued that "capital punishment is our way of demonstrating the sanctity of life."

630. New Hampshire House Speaker William O'Brien has stated that college students should not be able to register to vote on Election Day because they tend to vote liberal.

631. Contrary to what Republicans on the Congressional Education and the Workforce Committee say, Libby Nelson at Inside Higher Ed asserts that the government stands to profit off of student loans that Republicans in Congress refuse to police more: "[T]he government now keeps the difference, channeling some of the profits into financial aid programs and most of the rest toward deficit reduction (with some even flowing to administration priorities like early childhood education, as in the 2009 healthcare law). Once more direct and bank-based loans

are consolidated, and when the student loan interest rate increases to 6.8 percent next year (when a several-year effort to halve the rate ends), federal student loans will become even more lucrative for the government."

632. While most banks receive a mere 10 percent on overdue credit card bills, the U.S. Department of Education expects to get 85 percent of defaulted student loans.

633. While Rick Santorum promotes for-profit colleges (and criticizes Obama for waging war on them), they are under investigation for taking advantage of American veterans. Alex Horton, Iraq veteran and blogger at the Department of Veterans Affairs tasked with investigating the targeting by for-profit colleges on veterans' GI Bill money, says, "Take a look at the CEOs and directors of those for-profit schools, Kaplan, DeVry, Ashford. Where'd they go to school? Harvard, Stanford, Oxford. Zero are for-profit graduates."

634. In 2008, GOP lawmakers booed a group of high school students—the Charlottesville Young Liberals—who were visiting the Capitol to witness a session of the House.

635. GOP candidate Mitt Romney has mentioned plans to completely eliminate the Department of Housing and Urban Development.

636. Blatantly ignoring the first amendment, Senator Jim DeMint (R-SC) attempted to pass legislation that would ban discussing abortion over the internet.

637. In 2011, Michigan Republicans attempted to pass legislation that would imprison union members for sending emails that were political in nature.

Immigration

638. In trying to sway some Latino voters away from the Democrats, Republicans tried passing a more moderate immigration bill, but the backlash and revolt from their base caused Republican legislators to swing back the other direction, towards much harsher anti-immigrant policy.

639. In 2011, Republican State Rep. Virgil Peck of Kansas suggested a possible method of controlling illegal immigration similar to that of controlling feral hog populations— hunters in helicopters shooting at potential immigrants.

640. Republican Barry Wong, a candidate for the Arizona Corporation Commission, an elected body that decides public utility issues, wants to require the utility companies to check the immigration status of all customers, telling the press, "I'm sure there will be criticism about human-rights violations. Is power or natural gas or any type of utility we regulate, is that a right that people have? It is not a right. It is a service."

641. 2004 Republican platform on immigration key points:

    • Using biometric data to better track foreign travelers.

    • Amnesty encourages illegal immigration.

    • Reform and toughen immigration system to emphasize family.

    • Focus immigration on needed skills like agricultural work.

642. Former Republican Governor Arnold Schwarzenegger was an illegal immigrant for an extended period of

time, working as a bodybuilder and briefly as a brick-layer prior to receiving the special Visa necessary for an immigrant to do so.

643. Republican State Senator Russell Pearce of Arizona sponsored the *Support Our Law Enforcement and Safe Neighborhoods Act* (Arizona SB 1070) that, when passed in April 2010, would become the broadest and strict-est anti-immigration legislation in the nation's history. Opponents of the law equate it to "racial profiling" citing how the law targets Latinos and allows police officers to request proof of legal residency at the threat of a criminal charge, imprisonment, and deportation.

644. Michele Bachmann has been quoted saying, "I would build a fence on America's southern border on every mile, on every yard, on every foot, on every inch of the southern border. I think that's what we have to do, not only build it, but then also have sufficient border security."

645. Chairman Lamar Smith (R-Texas) criticized the Obama administration rules intended to prevent sexual abuse and inhumane conditions at Immigrations and Customs Enforcement facilities, claiming they made detention "too fancy."

646. Rep. Elton Gallegy (R-Calif.) recently compared immi-gration detention facilities to "college campuses."

647. Rep. Steve King (R-Iowa) has been recently quoted claiming "110 deaths is not alarming to me," referring to the number of detainees who died while awaiting deportation, not taking into account that the major-ity of these detainees were young and healthy prior to incarceration.

648. Republican condemnation of undocumented immigrants is nothing new, but Senator Marco Rubio's opposition to the DREAM Act—a piece of legislation that allows immigrants serving in the military or enrolling in college to work their way to citizenship—goes a step further. Rubio would allow these immigrants to remain in the U.S., but would prevent them from becoming citizens. In effect, Rubio favors creating a group of second-class Americans who could live and work in the country, but could never hope to vote or obtain a passport.

649. Representative Dana Rohrabacher (R-CA) spread misinformation about the DREAM Act, saying that it would put children of immigrants "ahead of every American child who's not a minority." Caught up in the racist undertones of his misinterpretation of the legislation, Representative Rohroabacher neglected to point out that the DREAM Act also reduces the deficit, strengthens the military, and helps to enforce immigration laws.

Race/Gender

650. According to political pundit Kevin Drum, Republicans are hesitant to take race issues seriously, often defaulting to the argument that liberals bring it up too often, instead of acknowledging the idea that racism against ethnic minorities is still a genuine and important issue in America.

651. Prominent Republicans from Reagan to Gingrich link government dependency and wasteful spending with Democrats and social services such as "food stamps" to "welfare queens" and minority communities; Gingrich

goes as far as to refer to President Obama as the "food stamp President."

652. In response to the shooting of Trayvon Martin in 2012—a seventeen-year-old, unarmed, African American boy—Newt Gingrich, Rush Limbaugh, and various other Republican voices rejected any suggestion that there were even racial issues to be discussed, jumping from the idea that race relations in this country have improved to the claim that black Americans no longer have any policy concerns worth discussing.

653. Rep. Sally Kern, R-Oklahoma City, has been quoted implying minorities generally earn less than their white counterparts simply because they don't work as hard and have less initiative: "We have a high percentage of blacks in prison, and that's tragic, but are they in prison just because they are black or because they don't want to study as hard in school? I've taught school, and I saw a lot of people of color who didn't study hard because they said the government would take care of them. [And women earn less than men because] they tend to spend more time at home with their families."

654. Right-wing zealot Phyllis Schlafly claims, "The feminist movement is the most dangerous, destructive force in our society today . . . . My analysis is that the gays are about 5% of the attack on marriage in this country, and the feminists are about 95% . . . . I'm talking about drugs, sex, illegitimacy, drop outs, poor grades, run away, suicide, you name it, every social ill comes out of the fatherless home."

655. Newt Gingrich: "And so I'm prepared if the NAACP invites me, I'll go to their convention and talk about

why the African-American community should demand paychecks and not be satisfied with food stamps."

656. Romney has said that he is not sure whether he will support the Lilly Ledbetter Fair Pay Act, which fights wage discrimination based on gender.

657. The College Republicans of Roger Williams University offer a scholarship for which only white students are eligible.

How Women Fit into the Republican Social Agenda

658. Rush Limbaugh, right-wing celebrity personality, claimed that government funding of female contraception equated to women, a law student named Sandra Fluke in particular, being prostitutes, stating, "It makes her a slut, right? It makes her a prostitute."

659. Arizona state representative Debbie Lesko has sponsored a bill that would essentially penalize women for using birth control for "non-medical" reasons, particularly pregnancy prevention.

660. An appointee of President George W. Bush, Federal Judge James Leon Holmes has claimed: "Concern for rape victims is a red herring because conceptions from rape occur with approximately the same frequency as snowfall in Miami"—effectively and erroneously equating rape itself to a form of contraception.

661. According to Shenna Bellows at the *Portland Press Herald*, the GOP-fueled debate over the government's right to

control women's reproductive rights "seems manufactured. When 99 percent of American women [and 98 percent of Catholic American women] use birth control, it stretches the imagination to call it controversial."

662. Republican Nancy Barto sponsored a bill in the Arizona Senate that protects physicians from malpractice, so-called "wrongful birth" lawsuits, when they neglect to inform pregnant women of prenatal problems that could have led to the decision to have an abortion. The Senate approved the bill with a 20-9 vote in March 2012.

663. In a public service announcement by Candie's Foundation to combat teen pregnancy, Sarah Palin's daughter Bristol opens, incongruously enough, by showing viewers a *positive* image of teenage pregnancy's ends; Bristol sports a pearl necklace, salon-styled hair, and a blazer ensemble befitting the daughter of a politician while she holds her infant son Tripp in a nicely decorated living room and says, "What if I didn't come from a famous family? What if I didn't have their support? What if I didn't have all these opportunities?" The scene changes to her in a ponytail, white T-shirt, and jeans in a Spartan apartment with Tripp as she says, "Believe me, it wouldn't be pretty." She then adds, "Pause before you play," the implied next phrase being, "but only if you don't have money and fame like I do to make teen parenting hunky-dory."

664. Republican Governor Scott Walker of Wisconsin recently repealed the state's Equal Pay Enforcement act of 2009, which provided ways for citizens to fight wage discrimination. The move leaves workers, women in particular, vulnerable to unfair pay and treatment in the workforce.

665. At the same time, Gov. Walker signed bills into law that would force schools to teach abstinence-only sex education; mandate that doctors consult privately with women seeking abortions; block any coverage for the procedure through the women's health care providers; and limits the expansion of a Wisconsin education voucher program so that many students would be prohibited from going to higher quality private schools.

666. In 2012, Wisconsin state Senator Glenn Grothman introduced a bill that would classify single parenthood as a form of illegal child abuse.

667. A Republican state legislator in Georgia wants to make the legal term for victims of rape, stalking, and domestic violence "accuser," while victims of other less gendered crimes, like burglary, would remain "victims."

668. In 2011, a Republican-backed proposal to legalize the murder of doctors who provide abortions on the grounds of justifiable homicide made its way to the South Dakota House.

669. Rep. Chris Smith (R-NJ) included in a 2011 proposed bill to exempt some rape victims from seeking federal help to pay for abortions the phrase "forcible rape" in a callous attempt to redefine rape and remove victim rights.

670. A Republican-sponsored bill, the Protect Life Act, aims to allow hospitals to let women die instead of performing an abortion.

671. A GOP lawmaker in Virginia advocating that women seeking an abortion undergo transvaginal ultrasounds beforehand recently defended her stance by claiming that

the women already decided to be "vaginally penetrated when they got pregnant." Democrats argue that the proposed law is essentially state sponsored rape.

672. Evangelist and 1988 Republican Presidential hopeful Pat Robertson said: "[Feminism] is about a socialist, anti-family political movement that encourages women to leave their husbands, kill their children, practice witchcraft, destroy capitalism and become lesbians."

673. Larry Pittman (R-NC) has stated that he not only supports the death penalty, but would be in favor of public hangings for anyone guilty of "murder"—by Pittman's reckoning, this would include doctors providing abortions.

674. The entry on Conservapedia for "feminism" makes the ridiculous suggestion that all feminists are lesbians who don't like baking and "often condemn the God-Given order of gender roles, as laid out in the Holy Bible." Clearly the conservative inability to grasp the nuances of contemporary feminism and its goals indicates that Republicans do not have women's best interests at heart.

675. Mitt Romney promised to overturn Roe v. Wade, calling it "one of the darkest moments in U.S. history."

Religious Discrimination:

676. In regards to religion's role in politics, Texas State Republican Executive Committee (SREC) member John Cook has been quoted saying: "I want to make sure that a person I'm supporting is going to have my

values. It's not anything about Jews and whether I think their religion is right or Muslims and whether I think their religion is right ... I got into politics to put Christian conservatives into office. They're the people that do the best jobs over all."

677. On his disdain for religious pluralism, GOP congressional candidate Allen West has said: "[A]s I was driving up here today, I saw that bumper sticker that absolutely incenses me. It's not the Obama bumper sticker. But it's the bumper sticker that says, 'Co-exist.' And it has all the little religious symbols on it. And the reason why I get upset, and every time I see one of those bumper stickers, I look at the person inside that is driving. Because that person represents something that would give away our country. Would give away who we are, our rights and freedoms and liberties because they are afraid to stand up and confront that which is the antithesis, anathema of who we are. The liberties that we want to enjoy."

678. While campaigning for the 2012 presidency, Newt Gingrich claimed that the Democratic or Republican National Committees have to pay for Christmas cards sent out by the president because, supposedly, "no federal official at any level is currently allowed to say 'Merry Christmas.'" Gingrich made up this alleged ban to increase panic over religious freedom, rather than stating the fact that the parties pay for holiday cards because of tradition and Congressional postage rules.

679. Newt Gingrich is allied with Christian Dominionists such as Dutch Sheets, whose interests include creating "warriors that are ready to do whatever it takes to bring forth [God's] kingdom rule in the earth."

680. When Pastor Dennis Terry introduced Rick Santorum at an event on the campaign trail, said America "was founded as a Christian nation," and anyone who disagrees should "get out! We don't worship Buddha, we don't worship Mohammad, we don't worship Allah!"

681. While speaking to faculty and students at Ave Maria University in 2008, Rick Santorum claimed that Satan has "corroded...the institutions of America."

LGBTQ

682. Christopher Plante, the executive director of the National Organization for Marriage, has claimed that the majority of the state of Rhode Island is opposed to gay marriage despite the complete lack of evidence. He said, "Would I repeat that I believe the majority of Rhode Islanders don't want gay marriage? Yeah, I'll repeat that. Can I give you a definitive poll that shows that? No."

683. When asked if gay voters should support his candidacy, Newt Gingrich said that they should vote for Barack Obama. In other words, the Republican Party finds homosexuality so loathsome that its candidates would rather lose than be supported by gay Americans.

684. In 2004, Michele Bachmann claimed that being gay is "personal enslavement," and that, if same-sex marriage were legalized, "little children will be forced to learn that homosexuality is normal and natural and that perhaps they should try it."

685. Speaking about gay-rights activists, Michele Bachmann said, "It is our children that is the prize for this community."

686. Gary Bauer, president of conservative group American Values, claims that the "overwhelming majority of the American people think that marriage is between a man and a woman." But in fact, several recent polls conducted reveal that a majority of Americans favor legalizing gay marriage.

687. The organization Republicans Against 8, aiming to curtail any advancement of same-sex marriage in California, argues that the legalization of gay marriage (particularly through 2008's infamous Proposition 8) challenges their beliefs in individual liberty, social regulation, and perhaps most paradoxically, equality and fairness.

688. Dr. Keith Ablow, a conservative Fox News Network personality, has been awarded the title of LGBT Misinformer of the Year by the organization Media Matters for America, because of use of pseudoscience and false medical authority to distribute bigoted attacks against the LGBT community, including, but not limited to, claiming that transgendered individuals suffer from psychotic delusions and attacking the Girls Scouts for allowing transgendered children.

689. Greenwell Springs Baptist Church pastor Dennis Terry, who introduced Rick Santorum at a campaign event in Baton Rouge, believes: sexually transmitted diseases are God's punishment to homosexuals; gays are coming after your children and grandchildren; being gay is "simply a perversion;" "no human being has ever been born gay;" gay people can and should change. Not a wise ally to have if the candidate were to care about the LGBTQ and allies of his country, of which a not-so-insignificant portion of Americans (52 percent,

according to a 2012 poll by the Public Religion Research Institute) supported legalizing same-sex marriage.

690. In a 2012 CNN interview, Newt Gingrich refused to accept undeniable evidence that Catholic Charities were not in fact denying same-sex adoption in Massachusetts, D.C., choosing rather to believe that the legalization of same-sex marriage prevented children from being adopted.

691. When asked if he thought the Republican party "ought to consider" something like civil unions, Michael Steele, chairman of the Republican Party, replied immediately, "No, no, no," adding, "What are you, crazy?"

692. The Republican definitions "marriage" and "family" exclude any situation that does not include one mother and one father. This intolerance stigmatizes gay marriage and overlooks the 2 million American children currently being raised by LGBT parents.

693. The Republican-controlled Michigan Senate included a provision in an anti-bullying law that allows for anti-gay bullying if such actions arise from "sincerely held religious belief or moral conviction." In other words, hate speech against homosexuals is just fine in Michigan as long as you are a Christian.

694. Tennessee—historically a red state—similarly introduced anti-bullying legislation that allowed for hate speech if it is founded in a deeply-rooted philosophical or political belief. Republicans are basically using religion and Party-affiliation as sanctions for hate.

695. Senator Scott Brown (R-MA), the only Republican member of Massachussett's delegation, was also

the only one of the state's congressional delegation to refuse to appear in Dan Savage's "It Gets Better" video. Rep. Carl Sciortino (D-Medford) said of this refusal, "Sen. Brown's absence in our congressional delegation's video sends a message that he supports kids being bullied or harassed . . . . I'm asking him, as a senator for the commonwealth, to stand up and show some leadership on behalf of his LGBT constituents, our young people that are facing violence in our schools, our young people that are being bullied in our schools."

696. Dan Savage said of the Republican aversion to support the expanding "It Gets Better" movement that he as an individual is "not the IGB project," as it has grown worldwide to tens of thousands of supporters. He finds it interesting that "not a single GOP elected official can bring himself or herself to make a video, or participate in the creation of one. No GOP elected official can risk being seen letting bullied LGBT kids know that life isn't high school and that it will get better for them. it doesn't require signing off on the entire gay agenda (the president made a video, and he doesn't support gay marriage). No GOP elected can back the seemingly radical notion that LGBT kids shouldn't kill themselves, that they should have hope for their futures."

697. Christopher Barron, cofounder of GOProud, a new movement combining Republicanism and the LGBT perspective, describe the difficulties GOProud faces in pursuing the junction of these traditionally opposed groups: "We know—Jimmy [LaSalvia, GOProud cofounder] and I know—that there are words that get said that the left thinks are warm and fuzzy to people that actually automatically turns conservatives off.

Instantaneously." These include, with an eyeroll from Barron, "inclusion," "fairness," and, as LaSalvia added with a chuckle, "equality."

698. Cofounder of GOProud Christopher Barron said, "I know a lot on the nasty, anti-gay right think they're going to relitigate this again next year and come up with any different of a response—I've got news for them: This has been a P.R. disaster for them."

699. The American Conservative Union's board of directors decided that GOProud would not be allowed to cosponsor the 2012 Conservative Political Action Conference.

700. While the so-called "Tea Party Patriots" claim that their allegiance is based on ideas of low taxes and small government, moralizing politics are really at the heart of this Republican sect that currently dominates the GOP scene. In particular, the Tea Party has been often noted for its anti-gay bigotry, repeatedly calling the gay community "aberrations."

701. Only two Republicans in Congress supported the repeal of "Don't Ask, Don't Tell."

702. Right-wing author and journalist David Kupelian has accused the faculty of Ohio State University of "marketing evil" because of their support of two homosexual professors and their opposition to Kupelian's book, "The Marketing of Evil," which equates homosexuality with evil and argues that the change of American's perceptions towards homosexuality is due to marketing and brainwashing.

703. Americans for Truth (about Homosexuality) and group president Peter LaBarbera aim to"expose the homosexual activist agenda" according to their website, advocating that "homosexual practice is always wrong but that people can leave the homosexual lifestyle" and operating with significant political influence Washington and the state of Illinois, the organization's home base, in particular.

704. J. Matt Barber is policy director for cultural issues at Concerned Women for America (CWA), a prominent right-wing public policy women's organization with a focus on bringing "Biblical principles into all levels of policy." He firmly believes that gay rights activists have unfairly cast homosexuals as a disadvantaged minority through propaganda and asserts that "the homosexual lifestyle has nothing to do with civil rights."

Government Shutdown and Filibuster

705. In 2011, House and Senate Republicans used the threat of government shutdown over budget and Planned Parenthood funding debate.

706. In recent years, Senate Republicans utilize the filibuster so persistently to thwart proposals from Democrats, whether liberal in content or not, that the fundamental function of the Senate seems to have shifted towards combating inevitable filibustering.

CHAPTER NINE

LIES, PROPAGANDA, AND BROKEN PROMISES

When it comes to mudslinging, the Republicans wrote the book on it. We at PDR remember back to the 2004 election between President Bush and Senator Kerry. If you listened to the right's propaganda, Kerry was a "flip-flopper" and they attacked his military record. Below, we will sum-up both Bush and Kerry's military accolades:

John Kerry

Served in the Navy from 1966-1970
Volunteered to be sent to Vietnam

Received the Bronze Star
> (The Bronze Star medal is awarded to individuals who, while serving in or with the military of the United States, distinguish themselves by heroic or meritorious achievement while engaged in military operations involving conflict with an opposing foreign force.[1])

---

[1] United States Department of Defense: www.defense.gov

Received the Silver Star
> (The Silver Star medal is the third highest military valor decoration that can be awarded to a person serving in any capacity with the U.S. Armed Forces. It is the highest U.S. Military valor decoration that may be awarded to members of the armed forces of friendly foreign nations.[2])

Received the Purple Heart 3x
> (The Purple Heart recognizes those individuals wounded to a degree that requires treatment by a medical officer in action with the enemy or as the result of enemy action where the intended effect of a specific enemy action is to kill or injure the service member.[3])

George Bush

Served in the Texas Air National Guard from 1968-1973
Transferred to inactive duty in the Air Force Reserve, honorably discharged in 1974
Requested not to be sent to Vietnam

With that information, you would think that Kerry would be praised as a war hero and Bush as someone who served, but never left the country. However, if you remember the election, it was pretty much the opposite. The right wing and Fox News bashed Kerry and tried to smear his military name, when all the while it was Bush who had the questionable military career.

Now we all saw how that ended, but that's just the beginning. The Republicans have been doing this for decades, and as you'll see, they have no signs of slowing down.

---

[2] United States Department of Defense: www.defense.gov
[3] United States Department of Defense: www.defense.gov

Historical Facts that Republicans Distort .

707. Sarah Palin has in the past made the false claim that Paul Revere's historical ride was intended to warn the British, when in fact, he warned the Americans of the British arrival.

708. Michelle Bachmann tired to convince a New Hampshire audience during her brief Presidential candidacy that the infamous first shot of the American Revolution occurred in New Hampshire, instead of where Lexington and Concord actually are located: Massachusetts.

709. Bachmann has also included President John Quincy Adams as a founding Father when he was in fact a small child when America was being founded.

710. Despite Republican claims to the contrary, America was not founded as a Christian Nation. In fact the complete opposite is true as evidenced in the First Amendment and throughout the Founding Fathers' recorded discourse.

711. Many Republicans have claimed that Benjamin Franklin rejected the theory of evolution. Two distinct problems arise from this claim: the theory of evolution, as expounded by Charles Darwin in 1859, had not existed in Franklin's time; and Franklin was a devout man of science above all else, even rejecting many aspects of the dogma of Christianity.

712. Evangelical conservative David Barton has claimed that the American Revolution was fought in part to end slavery in another attempt to paint the Founding

Fathers as perfect. The fact that slavery existed before, after, and during the war certainly refutes his claim.

713. Similarly, many Republicans claim the Civil War had been fought over state's rights, with no regards to the institution of slavery. Historical evidence and learned historians persistently deny this claim.

714. Republicans often claim that there exists a constitutional right for a state to secede from the Union, as done in the past, notably during the period leading up to the Civil War. Particularly after Obama took office, this sentiment has existed in many prominently Republican southern states, despite the fact that it is undoubtedly unconstitutional and has been rejected by both James Madison and Andrew Jackson (both southerners) in the past.

715. Rick Santorum has made the absurd claim that American soldiers stormed the beaches of Normandy during World War II to fight against President Obama's health care plan. "[Obamacare] is spitting in the face of those Americans who fought on D-Day, 67 years ago today," he argued in 2011.

716. The claim by the right-wing that Ronald Regan never raised taxes is flatly wrong. Reagan actually raised taxes every year from 1981 to 1987 including The Tax Equity and Fiscal Responsibility Act of 1982 which, at the time, had been the largest peacetime tax increase in U.S. history, the Deficit Reduction Act of 1984, a higher gasoline levy, a higher payroll tax, and a 1986 tax reform deal that included the largest corporate tax increase in American history.

717. Fox News host Eric Bolling actually claimed on air in 2011 that no terrorist attack occurred on American soil in 2001: "We were certainly safe between 2000 and 2008—I don't remember any terrorist attacks on American soil during that period of time."

718. Although Republicans argue federally mandated healthcare is unconstitutional, Congress passed and Vice President John Adams signed a mandatory health care insurance law back in 1791.

719. Republicans fight for a small, weak federal government allegedly called for by the constitution, despite the document itself and the history surrounding its creation. Before the current constitution, the United States operated under the Articles of Confederation and a smaller, weaker federal government. The U.S. Constitution in many ways exists to remedy that situation.

720. Republican politicians and pundits love to claim that 47 percent of American do not pay taxes. However, this claim was based on the fact that 47 percent of Americans did not have to pay federal income tax in 2009, and the statistic does not take into account federal payroll tax, sales tax, property tax, and state income tax that all Americans are required to pay.

721. The Republican battlecry has long been that American people and businesses pay far too much in taxes. However, taxes are currently the lowest they have been since 1958, and the U.S. has the third-lowest tax rate of all developed nations.

722. One of the biggest GOP fallacies is that taxes are right the way they are and shouldn't be raised (especially on

the wealthy), even while baby boomers retire and add extra weight onto Social Security and Medicare and the wealth gap increases.

Misguided Republican Ad Campaigns and Propaganda

723. Restore Our Future—the Super PAC backing Romney—has so far spent $39 million on ads attacking his rivals and a mere $1 million on positive ads in support of Romney. This is just another example of the Republican Party's tendency to favor smear campaigns over legitimately winning over American voters.

724. Despite Republicans blaming Obama for high gas prices, statistics from the U.S. Energy Information Administration show that gas prices spiked to $4.11 during the week of July 7, 2008, when Bush was president. This figure is higher than the highest price ($3.96, the week of May 16, 2011) during Obama's presidency as of April 2012.

725. The American Energy Alliance, a nonprofit group with Republican ties, has been blasting Obama's energy policy with a $3.6 million TV ad campaign in the eight states crucial for the general election, claiming unfairly of gas prices doubling.

726. The American Energy Alliance as well as Crossroads GPS, another pro-Republican interest group running a hateful TV ad campaign against Obama's energy policies and relationship with big oil in New Mexico, Ohio and Nevada, costing an estimated $650,000, are both funded by conservative billionaire oil company magnates Charles and David Koch, who have pledged more than $200 million to defeating Obama.

727. Mitt Romney claims, "We're inches away from no longer having a free economy" under Obama. However, conservative think tank Heritage Foundation provides some of the strongest evidence to the contrary, as the U.S. ranks low in total tax burden and high in economic freedom compared to the rest of the world.

728. Republicans including Mitt Romney oppose eliminating tax incentives and subsidies for the major U.S. oil companies, even as they report record profits, and in turn Big Oil finances ads smearing President Obama. A Democratic response ad even suggests that "The money they make from high gas prices is going right into Mitt Romney's campaign."

729. The Republican National Committee claims in ads that "Since President Obama Took Office The Nation Has Lost 1.9 Million Jobs" while the facts show since President Obama's policies took effect, the nation has gained over 1.9 Million jobs.

730. The tally in August 2010 according to economist Robert J. Shapiro is: Mr. Obama can be held accountable for the net loss of 41,000 jobs (671,000 - 630,000), while the Republicans should be held responsible for the net losses of 7,796,000 jobs.

731. The Republican National Committee claim in ads that "President Obama Has Racked Up The Three Largest Deficits In U.S. History" but the fact is that it's evident to economists and experts that Bush-era Policies spurred today's massive debt and deficits.

732. In television and radio and print ads the RNC claim that President Obama has failed to make health care

more affordable, when the truth reveals that health care reform has not raised rates significantly and has ensured more young people are receiving health coverage because of The Affordable Care Act—2.5 million between Americans aged 19-25.

733. During the 2004 Presidential election, Republican advisor Karl Rove orchestrated a campaign of phone calls, direct mail, and email in the Bible Belt claiming that Democratic nominee John Kerry intended on banning the Christian Bible in America if elected President.

734. Also during that election, a group financially backed by Bush supporters created a TV ad campaign smearing and discrediting the impressive military of Sen. John Kerry, a Navy hero with three Purple Hearts.

735. From around 2002 to 2005, the Bush administration has used federal funds to pay several journalists (including Washington Post syndicated columnist Maggie Gallagher) to write positively about Republican policies including their $300 million initiative to encourage marriage as a way of strengthening families.

736. Republicans in the state of Michigan recruited actors to run as phony Democratic candidates for nine state Senate seats. Luckily, the Muskegon Chronicle exposed the plan before it could be acted out on.

737. The "Arkansas Project" funded by both billionaire Republican Richard Mellon Scaife and more than $25 million of taxpayer funds, was created with the sole purpose of ending the Clinton presidency with scandals such as "Whitewater" and "Troopergate", linking Clinton with Pablo Escobar, and exploiting Clinton's extramarital affairs as much as possible.

738. Conservatives also claimed that, in 2007, Congress banned incandescent light bulbs, an apparent assault on American freedoms. But, Congress did no such thing.

739. Former House Speaker Newt Gingrich urged campaigning Republicans to contrast the Republican Party as the party of "paychecks" against Democrats as the party of "food stamps" in a memo he circulated in 2010.

740. In 1994, Rick Santorum was quoted blaming single mothers for ruining the country. He said, "Most people agree a continuation of the current [welfare] system will be the ruination of this country. We are seeing it. We are seeing the fabric of this country fall apart, and it's falling apart because of single moms."

741. Conservapedia's definition of "socialism" insists that modern socialism is tantamount to Nazism. This claim is obviously false and confuses the economic theory of socialism with the political ideology of fascism.

742. Michele Bachmann insisted that John Quincy Adams was one of America's Founding Fathers who worked to end slavery. In fact, it was his father, John Adams, who was a Founding Father, and John Quincy Adams died in 1848, fifteen years before the Emancipation Proclamation.

743. One of the many falsehoods Republicans have spread is that Democrats have asked for a $3.8 trillion tax increase, when in truth,the Republicans are referring to the Bush tax cuts that contain several provisions which Democrats oppose but even the repeal all of the Bush tax cuts would only amount to $3.1 trillion in taxes over ten years, all aimed at the substantially wealthy. The Democrats want no where near that much anyway.

744. Republican Senator Jon Kyl and several like-minded Republicans like John Boehner wholeheartedly insist that tax cuts, particularly those to businesses, "never have to be offset," as if they pay for themselves.

745. Despite the Republican propaganda campaign telling Americans that the Bush tax cuts did not add to the deficit and in fact increased revenue, the Center on Budget and Policy Priorities (CBPP) has made evidence public that shows the cuts causing a massive increase in the deficit during George W. Bush's tenure, and the tax cuts if made permanent would contribute more to the budget deficit than the Obama stimulus, the TARP program, the wars in both Afghanistan and Iraq, and the revenue lost to the recession … combined.

Misguided Republican Campaigns against Obama

746. Senator Mitch McConnell (R-KY) has stated that since 2008, "The single most important thing we want to achieve is for President Obama to be a one-term President." This proves that Republicans are more devoted to partisan politics than creating policy that actually helps America.

747. The Republican-tied nonprofit group known as the American Energy Alliance launched a $3.6 million TV ad campaign entitled "Nine dollar gas," which criticizes President Obama for his energy policy and blames him (and his avoidance to expand controversial oil and drilling projects like the Keystone pipeline) for the rising gas prices. Republicans shut down Obama's proposal to repeal $4 billion in subsidies in the oil industry, and instead they assert that a tax hike on oil companies would raise the price of gas for consumers. However,

giving oil companies motivation to drill elsewhere is not the answer, as "Drill Here, Drill Now, Pay Less" is rejected as a political ploy that ignores the historical and mathematical evidence that more U.S. drilling alone makes little impact on the world market of gasoline.

748. Mark Hemingway of the *Weekly Standard* took a photo of outrageously high gas prices (approaching $6) listed at the Watergate Exxon station, well-known to D.C. locals for ripping off tourists who don't realize nearby gas stations offer more reasonable prices. He jokingly titled it, "The Shocking Photo the Obama Administration Doesn't Want You to See!" but conservatives missed the joke; Glenn Beck republished the photo on his website The Blaze with the headline: "Inconvenient Photo Taken at Exxon Gas Station Just Outside White House." While Republicans jumped on the chance to blame Obama for the photo's evidence of rising gas prices, Jason Linkins at the Huffington Post revealed that at the Sunoco across the street from the Watergate Exxon, regular gas was just $4.10.

749. Republicans were in a frenzy over Obama's "National Defense Resources Preparedness" order, which was issued in March 2012 and permits the federal government to identify "requirements for the full spectrum of emergencies, including essential military and civilian demand." *Washington Times* writer Jeffrey Kuhner described this as "a sweeping power grab that should worry every American" that "one would expect to find in Hugo Chavez's Venezuela or Vladimir Putin's Russia." But contrary to the right-wing's panicked reasoning, Karl Manheim, professor of law at Loyola Law School Los Angeles, says that "If Canada invaded us and decided they were going to take over some of the Gulf

Islands off of Vancouver, then yes, the president could declare martial law by executive order. Otherwise, no, the president cannot simply defy Congress and declare martial law on his own."

750. Republicans assessed as a tactical advantage the fact that when Obama and the Democrats came into power, they inherited the worst economic crisis in eighty years. They have used this as fuel for propaganda to regain power, rather than using the facts to improve the situation for Americans.

751. A Republican myth was propagated in 2010 by chain emails and bloggers that all real estate transactions will be subject to a 3.8 percent sales tax thanks to Democrats: "Under the new health care bill—did you know that all real estate transactions will be subject to a 3.8 percent Sales Tax? The bulk of these new taxes don't kick in until 2013 (presumably after Obama's re-election). You can thank Nancy, Harry and Barack and your local Democrat Congressman for this one." However, the 3.8 percent tax only applies to couples who make over $250,000 or individuals making more than $200,000, less than 5 percent of all tax payers.

752. Mitt Romney has suggested time and again that the Obama presidency has led to a weaker military, smaller Navy, and lighter Air Force than that of fifty to 100 years ago. The comparison is dubious, being that military technology has advanced so far with regards to drones and nuclear weaponry, and is misleading since the United States is still unquestionably the world's military leader.

753. While campaigning for the 2012 presidency, Newt Gingrich deemed Obama "the most successful food

stamp president in American history." He also made the absurd statement that "We have people who take their food stamp money and use it to go to Hawaii . . . . You know, the Obama model: isn't there somebody you'd like to give money to this week."

754. While campaigning for the presidency, Mitt Romney claims that "a few months into office, (President Barack Obama) traveled around the globe to apologize for America." Not only did the president never once say the word "sorry" during these alleged forums for apologies, but also they represented Obama's promised different foreign policy approach to Bush's unilateralism.

755. Michele Bachmann also said in 2011 while campaigning for the presidency, "President Obama has the lowest public approval ratings of any president in modern times." Actually, Obama's lows are higher than most presidents' lows.

756. Conservapedia's entry for President Barack Obama maintains that he is a Muslim born in Kenya, while both of these claims have been proven repeatedly to be false.

757. Many Republicans asserted that the Affordable Care Act was intended to make Americans dependent on the government and to brainwash them into becoming future Democrats.

758. Mitt Romney claims Obama's campaign for re-election is based on "a platform of higher taxes" for the middle class (though of course, in following the Republican trend of rarely saying the phrase "middle class," he used the phrase "small businesses and job creators"). However, President Obama has cut taxes for virtually all working families, providing at least $3,600 in tax cuts over four years for the typical household.

Obama as an Elitist

759. An entry on *Conservapedia*, the conservative alternative online encyclopedia, entitled "Barack Obama and liberal elitism" begins, "Barack Obama has consistently shown himself to be a liberal elitist who looks down on 'ordinary' Americans."

760. A 2010 *Washington Post* column by Michael Gerson, the former speechwriter for President George W. Bush, was headlined simply "Obama the snob."

761. Conservatives jumped to label President Obama as an elitist when Obama remarked in 2010 that "facts and science and argument [do] not seem to be winning the day all the time is because we're hard-wired not to always think clearly when we're scared." However, labeling Obama as elitist ignores the facts of his single-mother upbringing (who once needed food stamps) and the work he had to do to pay off his college loans.

762. Anita Dunn, a Democratic strategist who advises Mr. Obama: "The elitism argument is kind of a false one because the president talks about people's economic interests and middle-class families. And those who are supporting Republican candidates right now—because they think they'll look out for their interests—are going to be very surprised when they find out what the corporate sponsorship of that party is buying."

763. During the 2008 presidential election campaign, Obama received much flack from Republicans for calling working-class Americans "bitter" and "cling[ing] to guns or religion." Meanwhile, Senator John McCain couldn't even remember the number of homes he owned.

764. Republicans erroneously claimed that President Obama's late 2010 trip to India would cost $200 million per day, or $2 billion for a ten day visit.

Obama's Religion Brought into Question

765. Chris Mooney, author of *The Republican War on Science* and *The Republican Brain: The Science of Why They Deny Science and Reality,* writes in an article at Mother Jones: "Many conservatives believe President Obama is a Muslim. A stunning 64 percent of Republican voters in the 2010 election thought it was 'not clear' whether he had been born in the United States. These people often think he was born in Kenya, and the birth certificate showing otherwise is bunk, a forgery, etc. They also think this relatively centrist Democrat is a closet—or even overt—socialist. At the extreme, they consider him a 'Manchurian candidate' for an international leftist agenda."

766. At a town hall in Florida in January 2012, a woman was cheered when she spoke up at a Rick Santorum campaign event to say that President Obama "is an avowed Muslim. Why isn't something being done to get him out of the government?" Instead of correcting her, Santorum responded, "Yeah, I'm doing my best to try to get him out of the government."

767. According to the Pew Research Center for the People and the Press, an August of 2010, "Roughly a third of conservative Republicans (34 percent) say Obama is a Muslim, as do 30 percent of those who disapprove of Obama's job performance."

768. Conservative propaganda questioning Obama's religion works, as a March 2012 Public Policy Polling survey of

Republican voters in Alabama revealed with the question asked, "Do you think Barack Obama is a Christian or a Muslim, or are you not sure?" The results: a mere 14 percent correctly believe Obama is Christian, 45 percent believe he is Muslim, and 41 percent are "not sure."

769. Rick Santorum propagated the confusion over Obama's religion when he said of Obama's agenda, "It's about some phony ideal, some phony theology. Oh, not a theology based on the Bible, a different theology. But no less a theology."

770. Republicans portray Obama as anti-Israel and criticize him for being weak against Islamic terrorism.

771. While campaigning in Georgia, Newt Gingrich said of Obama: "There's something sick about an administration which is so pro-Islamic that it can't even tell the truth about the people who are trying to kill us." (As John Feffer at Mother Jones aptly put it: "Pro-Islamic? That's news to the Islamic world.") Gingrich also deemed it "not possible" to "fix" Afghanistan, the citizens of which he advised to "figure out how to live your own miserable life."

772. Rev. Franklin Graham, a prominent evangelical leader, struggled in an interview on Morning Joe at NBC to explicitly endorse Obama's claim to Christianity. Rev. Graham said Obama "has said he's a Christian, so I just have to assume that he is." Later in the interview, he said that the Muslim world views Obama "as a son of Islam" because the president's father and grandfather were Muslim. Rev. Graham also added that "Islam has gotten a free pass under Obama."

773. Mitt Romney has said that Obama is against "religious liberty ... because of the people the president hangs around with, and their agenda, their secular agenda."

Broken GOP Promises

774. While the GOP pledged to "end the practice of packaging unpopular bills with 'must-pass' legislation to circumvent the will of the American people" and instead "advance major legislation one issue at a time," they broke this promise with the December 2011 passage of a law that extended the Social Security payroll tax cut and unemployment insurance. Bundled into this end-of-the-year legislation (thanks to House Republicans) was a sixty-day deadline for Obama to make a decision regarding the Keystone pipeline construction. Also bundled into this must-pass legislation was a provision that preempted the Environmental Protection Agency from applying pollution standards to industrial boilers.

775. In the GOP Pledge to America, Republicans promised to refrain from bundling unpopular bills with so-called "must pass" legislation and advance legislation one at a time. Nonetheless, Republicans continue to package unrelated items into legislation to get them through, including bundling a payroll tax extension late in 2011 with everything from the Keystone XL oil pipeline to the sale of broadband spectrum.

776. The GOP's pledge to America states that members "will ensure that bills are debated and discussed in the public square by publishing the text online for at least three days before coming up for a vote in the House of Representatives." However, Rep. Lynn Westmoreland (R-GA) lashed out at her fellow Republicans for the lack of transparency regarding the legislation to extend the federal debt ceiling: "after this deal was crafted behind closed doors with only a few members

of leadership at the table, we were given less than 12 hours to read and review this extremely important legislation. More time is needed to make an informed decision about legislation of this size and scope. Unfortunately, once again, Congress has waited until the last minute to act, pushing us up against this artificial August 2nd deadline and forcing a decision on a bill it seems no one actually likes."

777. In March of 2011, according to Politifact, "Republicans fast-tracked legislation to curtail funding for National Public Radio after Internet activist James O'Keefe distributed an edited video that appeared to show an NPR fundraising executive making disparaging remarks about the tea party movement, among other things. On Tuesday, House Republicans posted legislation to the Rules Committee website. On Thursday, they brought it to the floor and voted for it."

778. Republicans have often criticized the way Democrats bypass the rules of debate and avoiding an open amendment process in the House and promised to treat the Democratic minority different when they gained power. They haven't, claiming often that there's simply nothing to amend in GOP proposals and there's no need for the open amendment process that they had wanted prior and promised to enact.

779. Despites frequently touting a promise to cut $100 billion in spending, House Republicans now consider that number hypothetical and the actual figure has become significantly less.

780. The House GOP proposed a provision to make committee attendance open to the public in the name of

transparency, but would then secretly remove that provision in the name of laziness and concealment, using the excuse that hearings are often scheduled at the same time and Republican lawmakers wouldn't want to be criticized for missing hearings.

781. After requiring that all bills be fully paid for, the House Republicans made a special exemption for their own repeal of the health care reform law, which in itself goes against their promise to reduce the deficit since the health care law is designed to reduce the deficit by $143 billion by 2019, and the repeal bill will increase the deficit by $230 billion over the next ten years.

782. Republican lawmakers are opposed to federally funded health care but with the exception of very few (like Rep. Steve King of Iowa) they all enjoy federally funded health care.

783. The House Republicans' promise to focus on job creation after gaining the majority has been broken as of yet, with little time spent on legislation to create jobs or boost the economy. In fact, they're focus on bills to curb spending has in fact eliminated many jobs, potentially 7.4 million jobs if the proposals of House Republicans were signed into law.

784. The National Republican Senatorial Committee has claimed that the economic stimulus created "zero jobs," ignoring the actual numbers and evidence to the contrary. The Congressional Budget Office (CBO) says the bill lifted created or saved up to 3 million jobs.

785. Speaker of the House John Boehner has said, "So be it," in regards to the potential job losses that would come

from House Republican plans despite his previous claims to care about job creation, and strange opposition to the jobs President Obama has created.

786. Rep. Joe Walsh (R-IL) owed $117,000 in unpaid child support payments. Christian right-wing lobbying groups have praised and showered support on him nonetheless, including the Family Research Council, for his "unwavering support of the family."

787. Conservapedia came to existence as an alternative to Wikipedia when Andrew Schlafly discovered that the wiki was using BCE (Before Common Era) dating rather than BC (Before Christ) and decided that there needed to be a blatantly conservative leaning voice in the online encyclopedia realm—to attack evolution and claim homosexuality to be a choice tied to mental disorders.

788. Republican presidential candidate Mitt Romney has been repeatedly quoted as claiming, "[President Obama] went around the world and apologized for America," despite there being no reason to believe that as true.

789. Rick Santorum, in an attempt to paint the University of California schools as liberal and misguided, claimed that most of the public universities in the system did not offer courses on American history. The claim is brazenly false and easily proven so.

790. Republicans supporting the Keystone pipeline proposal have argued that President Obama's opposition equates to opposing job creation, but TransCanada, the Canadian company proposing the pipeline, has admitted that the project will only create thousands of temporary jobs, maybe hundreds of permanent U.S. jobs, and even those numbers are questionable.

791. Economist Mark Zandi has credited President Obama's 2010 payroll tax reduction with significantly helping to prevent recession. Still, Republicans like Michele Bachmann argue contrary to the professional wisdom in order to slander the president.

792. In regards to economics, Republicans hold the false beliefs that tax cuts equate to increased government revenue, the economic stimulus bill passed by President. Obama didn't work, and that the federal government can simply "prioritize payments" without raising the debt ceiling. This belief system is to the detriment of the American people.

793. Two House Republicans, Congressman Mike Fitzpatrick and National Republican Congressional Committee Chairman Congressman Pete Sessions, violated the Constitution on their first day in office in 2011 because they missed their swearing in. Instead, they were at a fundraiser in the Capitol Visitors Center, where they watched the swearing in from a television and raised their hands. Said Fitzpatrick of the missed swearing in, "That wasn't planned. It just worked out that way."

794. National Republican Congressional Committee Chairman Congressman Pete Sessions' website defined earmarks as "a symbol of a broken Washington to the American people." However, in 2008 he added a $1.6 million earmark for one of his former aides, Adrian Plesha, also a registered lobbyist (with a criminal record for Jim G. Ferguson & Associates) so the out-of-state company could research hi-tech blimps even though the president admits to having no experience in government contracting or dirigibles. Plesha has a

criminal record and has made $446,000 lobbying for Ferguson & Associates.

795. Mitt Romney pledged to shed any investments that might conflict with his political ethics, stating, "My trustee has indicated publicly that he will make an effort to make sure that my investments to the extent possible and practical, will conform with my political positions." However, Romney's company Bain Capital is still investing his money in China, while he publicly criticizes Obama for going too easy on China for human rights violations. Romney stands to benefit from the Chinese government's tools to intimidate and monitor political and religious dissidents.

CHAPTER TEN

WHAT LIBERALS ARE SAYING

Throughout this entire book, we've pretty much stayed away from speaking about the Democrats. The main reason: they're not in the title! But we thought we'd be doing an injustice to the other party if we completely left them out. Now, the Democrats aren't always the good guys. They've made a lot of questionable decisions and many mistakes; but the difference between these two parties is night and day. Not only do most Democrats disagree with many Republican decisions, but they speak openly of their distaste. While the red boys love to use smear tactics and have commercials and Fox News be their attack dogs, most Democrats, if you ask them, will tell you honestly what they think.

By listening to a Democratic debate, you quickly realize that while these candidates are competing against each other for the chance to run for president they all have the same common goal: to improve the country we all love so dearly. While they may not always agree on the same things, they're out for the best interest of the government and to improve everyone's way of living.

If you tune into a Republican debate, you'll see a full-fledged mud fight. They'll attack, yell, point fingers, and do everything they can to discredit their opponents. Now, we're not saying that the Democrats don't do this, but the intensity in which they do it and the Republicans do it are miles apart.

It seems to us here that the Democrats are as puzzled as the rest of the middle class at the way the Republicans are treating us. It really does not make sense to alienate a large group of Americans, but they continue to do so at every turn.

Quotes About Republicans

"In the most recent Republican primary debate, the word 'middle-class' once again was nonexistent."
—Anonymous progressive blogger

796. President Obama calls Paul Ryan's budget—which severely cuts Medicare funding, grants for college students, and early childhood education—"a prescription for decline."

797. Leading Darwinian Richard Dawkins on Mitt Romney's Mormonism: "I know those beliefs are private, but they're crazy beliefs. And why should I vote for a man, however sensible his public beliefs may be, if his private beliefs are ridiculous and mad?"

798. In response to the Ryan Republican budget plan, President Obama said, "It's really an attempt to impose a radical vision on our country. It's nothing but thinly veiled social Darwinism."

799. President Obama: "If you truly value families, you shouldn't play politics with a woman's health."

800. DNC Chair Debbie Wasserman Schultz thinks that her "Republican colleagues in Congress and Mitt Romney are rooting for economic failure . . . I mean, they've been hyper focused on one job, Barack Obama's, for really the last two years. And we all need to be pulling

together to focus on moving the economy forward for the middle class and for working families."

801. Vice President Joe Biden claims that Mitt Romney wants to let Detroit go bankrupt: Romney said that. He said what we propose, and I quote, "is even worse than bankruptcy." Bain Capital wasn't lining up to give anybody money. [Romney said] "the market, Wall Street, will help lift them out ... Wrong."

802. Al Gore state in an August 20, 2007, fundraisng letter: "For me, the most disturbing aspect of the Republican political culture is how it puts its unquenchable thirst for power, domination and a radical ideology above facts, reason and the truth."

803. On his January 31, 2012, show, Conan O'Brien said, "Studies are showing that Republican candidates are buying a lot of their ad time on the Weather Channel. You can tell because last night, the weatherman blamed the cold front on immigration and gay marriage."

804. "The Republicans . . . are having a hard time getting their members to act as a unit instead of like a bunch of six-year-olds playing anarchist soccer; three teams, two goals, you decide," said Rachel Maddow on *The Rachel Maddow Show* on February 15, 2011.

805. Michele Bachmann: "I made a misstatement."

806. "You've got the Bush Administration using [the September 11th attacks] in such a disrespectful and immoral way—using the deaths of those people to try and shred our civil liberties, change our Constitution, round people up. That's not how you honor them, by

using them to change our way of life as a free country," said Michael Moore in a CBS interview in June 2004.

807. "Politics, especially on the political right," says David Holtz, executive director of Progress Michigan, "is dominated by a cycle of money and favors. The hard-right conservatives who control Lansing and most of Washington these days are ideologically driven and corporate owned. They may or may not care about the middle class; I think motives are difficult to assess. But politicians are intensely focused on the short term, usually a two-year period or six at the most."

808. According to Democracy 21 President Fred Wertheimer, "Presidential candidate-specific super PACs are simply vehicles for circumventing the candidate contribution limits which were enacted to prevent the corruption of federal officeholders and government decisions. The findings of this study, showing that 84 percent of item-ized donors to the pro-Mitt Romney super PAC also gave the maximum legal contribution to the Romney presidential campaign, bear that out."

809. "I don't know what the middle class ever did to the Republicans that they're so out to get them," said former Speaker Nancy Pelosi, "but whether it's job cre-ation, economic growth, the tax code and the rest—the deck is getting stacked against the middle class."

810. Doug Pratt, public affairs director for the Michigan Education Association, wrote: "This isn't about politi-cal power or votes—it's about money for the corporate backers of the Republican agenda. Despite evidence from the fall of Rome to the Wall Street collapses (both in the

1920s and today) that a strong middle class is essential to over economic prosperity, there continues to be a greed-based mindset among many that 'less for them so there's more for me' is a good approach. Fact is, it's not. Ask any small business owner who is struggling today because there's less disposable income in our economy."

811. Author Chris Mooney has said, "The mid-2000s saw the mass dissemination of a number of falsehoods about the war in Iraq, including claims that weapons of mass destruction were found after the US invasion and that Iraq and Al Qaeda were proven collaborators. And political conservatives were much more likely than liberals to believe these falsehoods."

812. David Holtz, executive director of Progress Michigan, has recently said about Republicans, "While their policies shrink the middle class by holding down wages, financially starving schools and promoting policies that fatten corporate profits by driving jobs and investment offshore, they are rewarded in the short-term. The reward: campaign money . . . Until we drain the swamp of corporate cash our politics will continue to be polluted until all the oxygen is drained from our democracy."

813. "Mitt Romney's comment . . . that 'corporations are people' is one more indication that Romney and the Republicans on the campaign trail and in Washington have misplaced priorities. It is a shocking admission from a candidate—and a party—that shamelessly puts forward policies to help large corporations and the wealthiest Americans at the expense of the middle class, seniors, and students," said DNC chair Debbie Wasserman Schultz.

814. "Here's the basic outline of House Budget Committee Chairman Paul Ryan's 2013 budget in one sentence: Ryan's budget funds trillions of dollars in tax cuts, defense spending and deficit reduction by cutting deeply into health-care programs and income supports for the poor," says *Washington Post* contributor Ezra Klein.

815. *New York Magazine* contributor Jonathan Chait claims, "The Republican Party is in the grips of many fever dreams. But this is not one of them. To be sure, the apocalyptic ideological analysis—that 'freedom' is incompatible with Clinton-era tax rates and Massachusetts-style health care—is pure crazy."

816. From author Chris Mooney: "In one study, 37 percent of authoritarians (but 15 percent of non-authoritarians) believed WMD had been found in Iraq, and 55 percent of authoritarians (but 19 percent of non-authoritarians) believed that Saddam Hussein had been directly involved in the 9-11 attacks."

817. Representative Edward J. Markey, Democrat of Massachusetts, said the Republicans were giving gifts to "their planet-polluting patrons, Big Oil and Big Coal," and he asserted that "GOP used to stand for Grand Old Party. Now it stands for Gang of Polluters. Now it stands for Gas and Oil Party."

818. About the GOP's 2012 budget proposal, economics and politics blogger for the *New York Times*, Paul Krugman, has written, "What we learn from the latest Republican budget is that the whole pursuit of a Grand Bargain was a waste of time and political capital. For

a lasting budget deal can only work if both parties can be counted on to be both responsible and honest—and House Republicans have just demonstrated, as clearly as anyone could wish, that they are neither."

819. "[Republicans'] willingness to deny what's true may seem especially outrageous when it infects scientific topics like evolution or climate change. But the same thing happens with economics, with American history, and with any other factual matter where there's something ideological—in other words, something emotional and personal—at stake," says author Chris Mooney. "As soon as that occurs, today's conservatives have their own 'truth,' their own experts to spout it, and their own communication channels—newspapers, cable networks, talk radio shows, blogs, encyclopedias, think tanks, even universities—to broad- and narrow-cast it."

820. On the Keystone XL oil pipeline being bundled into the payroll tax cut, President Obama has accused House Republicans of abusing their power by protecting tax breaks for the wealthy and injecting "ideological issues into what should be a simple debate about cutting taxes for the middle class."

821. DNC Chair Debbie Wasserman Schultz, on the Fox News Republican Presidential debate: "Every candidate raised their hand tonight and pledged to not require millionaires, billionaires or the special interests to pay an additional dime to address our nation's problems—this in a debate where they didn't mention the middle class one time and continued to stand by plans like Cut, Cap and Balance, which would end Medicare as we know it."

822. President Obama criticized the GOP for their commitment to "trickle-down economics" saying, "It's a simple theory—one that speaks to our rugged individualism and healthy skepticism of too much government. It fits well on a bumper sticker. Here's the problem: It doesn't work." He continued, "It's never worked."

823. "For you, and for most Americans, protecting women's health is a mission that stands above politics. And yet, over the past year, you've had to stand up to [Republican] politicians who want to deny millions of women the care they rely on, and inject themselves into decisions that are best made between a woman and her doctor," reads the transcript of President Obama's address to women and Planned Parenthood. "Let's be clear here: Women are not an interest group."

824. Janeane Garofalo also stated: "I hate the right because they're all about thwarting people's potential. They hinder imagination and the ability to move forward toward enlightenment and modernity."

825. Garofalo also stated: "It's because of the right that we keep revisiting the same culture wars, militarism in all of its forms, and their version of manliness, which includes the lauding of anti-intellectualism. I mean, I can't believe we're talking about women's rights and gay issues again. We're even talking about the end of days again."

826. John Nichols, a pioneering political blogger, responds to Mitt Romney's allegation that Obama is against religious freedom: "The 'religious liberty' Romney referred to was a newly discovered 'constitutional right' to deny women access to contraceptives."

827. Paul A. Gigot at the *Wall Street Journal* wrote, "Republicans fiercely resisted NATO and other international entanglements, only to have them accepted in large part by the Eisenhower administration and later GOP presidents."

828. Reviewing Dick Cheney's book *In My Time*, Gigot also writes: "He also suggests the insider role that Alan Greenspan played in administration councils as chairman of the Federal Reserve. Mr. Greenspan endorsed Mr. Cheney's misguided advice to Mr. Bush to select Paul O'Neill as his first Treasury chief. Such closeness to the White House may explain why no one in the administration noticed that the Fed's easy money policy was producing a credit mania that led to surging oil prices, the housing bubble and ultimately to financial panic. Second note to GOP candidates: Keep your Fed chiefs at a prudent political distance."

829. Tom Malinowski at *Foreign Policy* wrote, in 2011, after Cheney's memoir came out that "torture has occurred in every war the United States has fought. Ethicists sometimes have considered whether there are exceptional circumstances under which individuals might be justified in violating domestic and international laws against torture. But prior to George W. Bush's administration, there was no debate in America about the legitimacy of the practice per se, any more than there was a debate about the legitimacy of rape or slavery. And the U.S. government had never before sought to give it legal sanction."

830. Larry Bartels, a Princeton political scientist, wrote in his 2008 book, *Unequal Democracy*, "The narrowly economic focus of most previous studies of inequality has caused

them to miss what may be the most important single influence on the changing U.S. income distribution over the past half-century—the contrasting policy choices of Democratic and Republican presidents. Under Republican administrations, real income growth for the lower- and middle-classes has consistently lagged well behind the income growth rate for the rich—and well behind the income growth rate for the lower and middle classes themselves under Democratic administrations."

831. Timothy Noah at *Slate*: "What did Democrats do right? What did Republicans do wrong? [Larry] Bartels doesn't know; in *Unequal Democracy* he writes that it would take 'a small army of economists' to find out. But since these are pre-tax numbers, the difference would appear to be in macroeconomic policies. (One clue, Bartels suggests, is that Republicans always worry more than Democrats about inflation.) Bartels' evidence is circumstantial rather than direct. But so is the evidence that smoking is a leading cause of lung cancer. We don't know exactly *how* tobacco causes the cells inside your lungs to turn cancerous, but the correlation is strong enough to convince virtually every public health official in the world."

832. Alex Parene of *Salon* wrote: "If Ronald Reagan was a genuine UFO nutter or simply in thrall to a simplistic sci-fi plot makes no difference to me. But the fact remains that he spent a *lot* of time talking about spacemen. Spacemen killed, according to my estimates, no Americans, at all, during Reagan's presidency."

833. "Reagan never mentioned AIDS until he was directly questioned about it in his second term, and he never

gave a public statement on the epidemic until 1987, when 20,000–30,000 people had already died from it."

834. Joy Behar: "Poor white people, poor black people are the ones who are oppressed by the right wing in this country, but they don't seem to get that. They vote against their own interests all the time."

835. Matt Lauer: "Is raising taxes on the table? … Why shouldn't the burden be equally shared? Why shouldn't we put some of that burden on the wealthy and corporations?"

836. George Monbiot, refuting the GOP claim that the 1 percent are wealthier because they work harder: "If wealth was the inevitable result of hard work and enterprise, every woman in Africa would be a millionaire."

837. Former Vice President Al Gore has said, "The single largest source of campaign financing for most of those (Republican) candidates is the oil industry and the coal industry."

838. Al Sharpton once said of the former president, "George Bush giving tax cuts is like Jim Jones giving Kool-Aid. It tastes good but it'll kill you."

839. In response to the debt ceiling threats made by Republicans in 2011, Al Gore wrote: "A significant number of Republican and Tea Party Members of Congress apparently hold the view that there actually would not be consequences for global markets or the U.S. economy if we defaulted."

840. Al Gore has stated that it is "absolutely the case" that Republicans are financed by fossil fuel industries and thus see it fit to play skeptical on climate change.

841. "Republicans rely on massive contributions from corporate special interests. But Democrats rely on your grassroots strength," Al Gore wrote recently in a letter on behalf of the Democratic Congressional Campaign Committee (DCCC).

842. Vice President Joe Biden claims the Republican Party is responsible for a severe divide in Washington. "I do think the idea of compromise is still alive and well with the Democrats and the Congress," he said in a recent *CBS News* interview. "But with enough of a minority in the Republican Party controlling the majority, there is no room for compromise. I mean none."

843. After Mitt Romney called Russia the "No. 1 geopolitical foe" of the United States during his presidential campaign, Secretary of State Hillary Clinton labeled his perspective, and the global perspective of those who think like him, "somewhat dated."

844. Joe Biden has said that the Republican stance on women's rights is "totally out of touch with reality" and emphasizes "the right of women to decide for themselves whether or not they want to use contraception."

845. Joe Biden has said that the 2012 Republican candidates would "bankrupt the middle class" if any were elected as president.

846. In 2012, Joe Biden told a crowd that the GOP will allow firefighters and policemen to die to protect the interests of the rich. "You're stuck in a God-awful mess, and so it doesn't make sense to us that [cuts to the police force and firefighting force] would be happening at a time when the need for y'all actually would be increasing," he said.

847. Secretary of State Hillary Clinton warned that Republican-proposed cuts in foreign aid will do harm to the country's national security. "Cuts of this magnitude will be devastating to our national security, will render us unable to respond to unanticipated disasters and will damage our leadership around the world," Mrs. Clinton said in a letter to a Republican Rep.

848. Hillary Clinton has told international audiences to ignore anything Republican presidential candidates have to say about foreign policy: "There are comments made that certainly don't reflect the United States, don't reflect our foreign policy, don't reflect who we are as a people."

849. Liberal journalist Rachel Maddow has attacked Michigan Republicans for fundamentally ignoring legal democratic processes in the state and eliminating the voting rights of Democrats at the local level, saying, "If you care about the idea that we still use voting here, we still use democracy. If you care about the constitution, frankly Michigan ought to have a flashing red siren on it right now."

850. Rachel Maddow has lambasted the Republican party and candidates for their apparent 2012 war on women and women's rights, saying, "Mitt Romney is campaigning saying that he would like to end all family

planning support at the federal level. He would like to eliminate federal Title 10. Rick Santorum says he would like states to be able to make contraception illegal." She continued, "You can try to make this an issue of 'oh, Democrats hate religion,' but … this is about providing health insurance and the Republican Party is waging war on contraception."

851. Former President Bill Clinton has criticized the Republican climate change skeptics, saying they're making the United States "look like a joke" and that voters should make it "politically unacceptable" to deny climate change.

852. President Bill Clinton has said that Mitt Romney's late father, former chief executive of American Motors and governor of Michigan, must be "rolling over in his grave" because of Romney's opposition to the auto industry bailout that could save millions of jobs.

853. "[The Republicans'] idea of compromise is if they get only 80 or 85 or 90 percent of what we want and the Democrats don't get any of what they want. Most Americans don't consider that a compromise," former President Bill Clinton said of the GOP's negotiation strategy.

854. "Be mad," Pres. Clinton said during a University of Kentucky speaking event in 2010. "[The Republicans] are playing you, and you know it."

855. "We're living in a time when the Republicans have only pushed harder and harder to the right," says President Clinton in 2012. "And every time the president adopts a plan that they once advocated, they

abandon it and push farther to the right. But the voters can push them back."

856. House Minority Leader Nancy Pelosi called the Republican backed Protect Life Act, which, among other things, would prevent accountability for health care providers who willfully let women die during abortions, "appalling." "Under this bill," Pelosi continues, "when the Republicans vote for this bill today, they will be voting to say that women can die on the floor and health care providers do not have to intervene, when this bill is passed."

857. "I think it's really curiouser and curiouser that as we get further into this debate, the Republican leadership of this Congress thinks it's appropriate to have a hearing on the subject of women's health and can purposely exclude women from the panel," Nancy Pelosi said during a 2012 press conference after Chairman Darrell Issa's (R-CA) refused to allow a woman to testify in favor of the Obama administration's contraception rule.

858. "Yes, it is bipartisan. We pledge to the flag. That's a big thing. We have a oneness about us in many ways," said Nancy Pelosi regarding the House Republican's 2012 JOBS Act that received a show support from the White House. She continued, "But let's not mistake it for what we need to do for a real, serious, comprehensive jobs bill for our country."

859. In regards to the recent Republican budget proposal, House Minority Leader Nancy Pelosi claims that Republicans clearly "don't support family planning."

She went on, "How could it be? How out of touch could they be? But now the public will see."

860. "They don't believe in a government role except when it comes to women exercising her conscience on an issue like that," Nancy Pelosi recently said. "People who choose to marry and find comfort with each other—they decide that government should step in there. But clean air, clean water, food safety, public safety, public education, public health, Medicare, Medicaid, Social Security—they want to end the government role."

861. House Minority Leader Nancy Pelosi has accused Republicans of using religious freedom as an excuse to harm women in their legislation against providing health and contraceptive services to women: "We shouldn't have to be to a place where people are saying—when the overwhelming practice is going in favor of women's health—'we want to pull that back.' And use the excuse of religious freedom, which, of course, this is not."

862. Michael Moore told Rachel Maddow in a recent interview that "[Republicans] hate anything that has to do with unions, autoworkers, African Americans ... Detroit."

863. Chicago Mayor and former White House Chief of Staff Rahm Emanuel said of Republican presidential hopeful Mitt Romney that he "turns a blind eye" to the struggles of the middle class and "revealed himself" as someone who doesn't take voters' values into account because he's generally "too far removed."

864. Rahm Emanuel has said the GOP refuses "to budge on a single piece of their agenda" which is "not how you get to an agreement." While Obama offers plans, Emanuel says, Republicans offer just "an ideology."

865. Rahm Emanuel has called all the Republicans running for President in 2012 "turkeys."

866. Political humorist Jon Stewart has called the 2012 Republican primaries essentially "a telethon for electoral dystrophy."

867. "It must be tough for Republicans to love America so much, but hate three-quarters of the people living in it," Jon Stewart said recently on his comedy news television program.

868. Liberal journalist Chris Matthews has accused the Republican Party of treating American women "like they're not really voters" with their recent policy proposals.

869. Chris Matthews claims that the GOP is fundamentally outsourcing the election to "the Mormon" Mitt Romney, hoping that he will able to beat Pres.Obama by taking advantage of the "religious prejudice is at work here" despite being "a guy they really think is the other."

870. New York Times columnist Maureen Dowd attacked the GOP for their misogyny: "The attempt by Republican men to wrestle American women back into chastity belts has not only breathed life into President Obama, it has roused and riled Hillary [Clinton]. And that could turn out to be the most dangerous thing the wildly self-destructive G.O.P. leaders have done."

871. "In some kind of insane bout of mass misogyny, Republicans are hounding out the women voters," liberal journalist Maureen Dowd writes in her New York Times column.

872. John & Elaine Mellencamp in "An Open Letter to America" said, "The Governor of California was removed from office based on finance troubles. And yet George W Bush has lied to us, failed to keep our own borders secure, entered a war under false pretense, endangered lives, and created financial chaos. How is it that he hasn't been recalled? Perhaps this time we could even have a real election . . . but that wouldn't fit the Bush administration's 'take what you want and fire people later' policy. Take an election; take an oil field; take advantage of your own people— a game of political Three-Card Monte."

873. Maureen Dowd writes, "The Republicans, with their crazed Reagan fixation, are a last-gasp party, living posthumously, fighting battles on sex, race, immigration and public education long ago won by the other side."

874. "[The 2002 Nobel Peace Prize] should be interpreted as a criticism of the line that the current [Bush/Republican] administration has taken. It's a kick in the leg to all that follow the same line as the United States," said Nobel Committee Chairman Gunnar Berge on giving Jimmy Carter the Nobel Peace Prize.

875. Former House Rep. Cynthia Mckinney led the charge in uncovering details about the Bush administration's handling of 9/11 and prior intel. She's been quoted saying "We know there were numerous warnings of the events to come on September 11th

. . . What did this administration know and when did it know it, about the events of September 11th? Who else knew, and why did they not warn the innocent people of New York who were needlessly murdered? What do they have to hide? Persons close to this administration are poised to make huge profits off America's new war."

876. About the war in Afghanistan, political activist Gore Vidal has said, "Well, he (Bush) might as well have been bombing Denmark. Denmark had nothing to do with 9/11. And neither did Afghanistan, at least the Afghanis didn't."

877. When asked why Republicans think it is acceptable to demonize President Obama and the poor to the extent that they have, Rev. Jesse Jackson has said, "... and then somebody shoots an AK-47 in the White House ... to demonize him and demonize the poor is unacceptable."

878. Rev. Jesse Jackson argues, "the whole Republican Party, all of the elitists are determined to support the 10th amendment—that's a state's right as sovereign, which means states have a right to determine who gets an education, who has the right to vote." He continues, "It's not so much what [a Republican] says, it's what they do. And what they do is seek to be indifferent to pain and possibilities of black people."

879. "Republicans are marching in virtual lockstep with banks and corporations in resisting reform," writes Jesse Jackson in an op-ed article for the progressive blog, the Huffington Post.

880. Actor Ed Asner said of Republicans, "They're sheep. They like him (Bush) enough to credit him with saving the nation after 9/11. Three thousand people get killed, and everybody thinks they're next on the list. The president comes along, and he's got his six-guns strapped on, and people think he's going to save them."

881. Ed Asner has bluntly challenged the issues that Republicans promote, claiming "the crap that's espoused as causes is shocking." He continued, regarding Republican policy promises, "If they implemented after they've spoken the way they have, then I really fear for this country."

882. Senator Al Franken of Minnesota believes that House Republicans "don't want people to get jobs before the election" so they intentionally slow down the procedural processes.

883. Democrat Al Franken displayed his mathematical prowess in a fundraising email in 2012. Enclosed was the equation: "X = President Romney. Y = a Republican Senate. X + Y = Z. Solve for Z. Z could mean the end of Medicare as we know it."

884. "We have seen what happens when Republicans take control of Congress with a Democratic president and it ain't pretty," Democratic Senator Al Franken said in 2010.

885. As Republicans continued their campaign against minority and female appointments to the Supreme Court, even bashing Thurgood Marshall and labeling him an activist, not a judge, Senator Al Franken defended Marshall and shed light on why several of the

decisions Republicans "seem to like"—Citizens United v. Federal Election Commission for example—are more akin to activism than any by Thurgood Marshall. He even highlighted Brown v. Board of Education as "an exemplar of overturning a precedent that needed to be overturned," not mere activism.

886. In a speech to labor unions in 2011, Al Franken said, "Senate Republican leadership has said that their number one goal is to ensure that Obama is a one-term president. They didn't say it's to put people back to work, they didn't say it is to get our kids educated. They didn't even say it's to balance the budget."

887. Obama has compared Republican economic proposals to failed science experiments: "If experiment fails badly, you know, you learn from that. Right? … but you don't then just keep on doing the same thing over and over again. You go back to the drawing board. You try something different."

888. Vice President Biden has attacked the GOP for the treatment of Medicare in their budget proposals that tend to favor the wealthy, claiming "The choice they made was, in order to 'save the program' they lowered the standard of living for those on Medicare rather than asking the wealthiest among us to help deal with the problem."

889. "Suppose you were an idiot. And suppose you were a Republican. But I repeat myself," said Harry S. Truman.

890. Frank Zappa: "Republicans stand for raw, unbridled evil and greed and ignorance smothered in balloons and ribbons."

891. Rachel Maddow: "Here's the thing about rights. They're not actually supposed to be voted on. That's why they're called rights."

892. Jesse Ferguson, spokesman for the Democratic Congressional Campaign Committee (DCCC):

893. "Republicans leaders have zero intention of carrying through on their zero-tolerance pledge for Republicans' ethics scandals and corruption. Each month it seems another scandal-plagued Republican is revealed. Republicans' top priorities are their special interest allies, ultra-wealthy campaign contributors, their campaign treasuries and their personal bank accounts—not the best interest of middle-class families and seniors."

894. Al Gore: "For me, the most disturbing aspect of the Republican political culture is how it puts its unquenchable thirst for power, domination and a radical ideology above facts, reason and the truth."

895. Maureen Dowd said, in reference to the Republicans Regan fixation, that they are "trying to roll back the clock, but time is passing them by."

896. President Obama said while campaigning for re-election, "Mitt Romney is the beneficiary of a broken tax system, and he wants to keep it that way"

897. President Obama mocked the GOP's outdated and intolerant views about American border control, saying, "maybe they'll need a moat. Maybe they'll want alligators in the moat."

From Everyday Folks: Thoughts on Republicans

898. Liberal college professor Paul Buchheit has said, "Progressive activists continue to work toward the day when poverty is down everywhere, and minorities receive equal treatment, and education is properly funded, and tax subsidies rather than entitlements are minimized. But that day is being delayed by make-believe messages from the American conservative."

899. Humorist Daniel Dickey has said, "The cardinal concern of the republican party is to insure that the rich stay wealthy. That is, always has been and always will be the most important matter for the right-wing. It's why major corporations—especially those that bring harm to society and the environment—offer so much financial support to republicans."

900. "50 Cent voted for George Bush. Do you think a one-time drug dealer and son of a crack head has anything other than money in common with the onetime owner of the Texas Rangers and son of the president?" asks Daniel Dickey. "He wasn't a republican before he was rich—hell, I'm not even sure he paid taxes before he was rich. He was a democrat and then after becoming a billionaire, became a republican."

901. A Wisconsin librarian and blogger has said, "In listening to Santorum / Gingrich / Romney / Catholic bishops, it is fun to measure just how far back they want to go. Santorum and the obvious culture warriors proclaim that it was the 60s that led everyone astray. Many seem to want to reinstate the pre-Depression

rules for banking and the stock market. Some venture into the Jim Crow era, which started the day the Civil War ended. Many of their policies and attitudes hark back to the Gilded Age of the Robber Barons and seem to welcome Dickens level poverty (are there no workhouses?)."

902. "If you're making upwards of $250,000 and your sole concern is to pay the least amount of taxes, yes, it fiscally makes sense to vote republican," says liberal humorist Daniel Dickey. "But in that, lies an issue. Most families are not wealthy." He goes on to ask, "So why would they ever vote for someone whose interest it is to help the rich and hinder the masses?"

903. Responding to Governor Rick Scott (R-FL) and his CEO-headed economic team's findings that the unemployed are lazy, don't actually look for work, and don't deserve federal relief, environmental activist Linda Young of the Clean Water Network said, "The message is, 'We are going to have a feeding frenzy on your natural resources and tax dollars, and you are going to have jack . . . to say about it, so get used to it,' "

CHAPTER ELEVEN

REPUBLICANS AS LAUGHING STOCKS

And now for something completely different! Throughout this book, we at PDR have taken a serious stand on the ridiculousness of the Republican Party. We have showed how they are continuing to hurt the middle class and care more about their ideologies and opinions than what's best for the country. If you put on Fox News, you'll see the constant mud-slinging by the right wing at anything liberal. But, while the right may monopolize that station, everywhere else in the media they are the butt of all the jokes. On late night television (Conan, Leno, Letterman, Fallon, Kimmel, SNL), Comedy Central (Stewart, Colbert), or HBO (Maher), the ridicule of the Republicans and what they're trying to do to this country is constantly scrutinized and absolutely ripped to shreds.

We all remember the constant jokes about President Bush; but the problem was that he made it <u>so easy</u>! One of our members took a trip to Europe during Bush's presidency, and at one point saw a container with the President's face on it. When he showed the cashier the container to say how he was American, the cashier responded, "Yes! He is our favorite monkey!" It's one thing when people here poke fun at our government, but when our government is the butt of other countries jokes, then there's obviously a problem.

While in this chapter we will poke fun at the Republicans and all the shenanigans they've pulled in the past, it's almost sad how easy some of these jokes are. You'll even see that some of the punch lines are not punch lines at all, but actual things these people have said!

Even though the Democrats get made fun of as well, the percentage is probably 85-15. It's a shame that this superpower is considered a joke to the rest of the world. As far as we've come, we're almost looked at as a backwards nation . . . and the Republicans are the ones who are leading that march.

Whether you laugh or sigh at these jokes, just remember that if the Republicans weren't so backwards in their thinking and the way they act, all the comedians and talk show hosts wouldn't have as much material.

Lucky for them, it seems as if they'll have materials for decades to come.

903. Jon Stewart tells Republicans that nominating Newt Gingrich would be a mistake: "I know you're mad ... der than usual. The county's being run by a foreign-born Hawaiian, radical Christian Muslim, socialist who's in the pocket of Wall Street. And sometimes Newt Gingrich can sound like the answer. Reagan had a certain charm and gentility. Gingrich is like what would happen if Reagan had been abandoned as a child, and raised by a family of cactuses."

904. Senator Tom Coburn (R-OK) protested a television broadcast of *Schindler's List* because of nudity, about which Jon Stewart commented, "That's what strikes you as obscene in *Schindler's List*?"

905. Senator John McCain accidentally endorsed President Obama while at a campaign rally for Mitt Romney.

He said, "I am confident, with the leadership and the backing of the American people, President Obama will turn this country around." Governor Nikki Haley (R-SC) grabbed McCain's elbow to correct him, as the crowd also expressed anger over McCain's faux pas. McCain corrected himself: "Excuse me, President Romney."

906. After showing an image of former President George H. W. Bush sitting next to Mitt Romney to support his bid for president in 2012, Jon Stewart at first compared the former president's appearance to that of Hugh Hefner. When he corrected himself, he pointed out that "the optics in this photo are important … It's Mitt Romney, and an almost ninety-year-old guy in what looks like formal yachtwear. But look at the picture. Who in it looks like the hipper, more relatable guy to hang out with? It ain't Romney! Romney's so bland in this picture, he makes Bush look almost ethnic."

907. Said Paul Ryan on Fox News: "The more we drag it out, the harder it is to win in November. I think we're entering a phase where it could become counterproductive if this drags on much longer. And so that's why I think we need to coalesce as conservatives around Mitt Romney." Adds Jon Stewart: "We have voted enough."

908. Senator Marco Rubio (R-FL) said, "Well, I am going to endorse Mitt Romney and the reason why is not only because he's going to be the Republican nominee but he offers such a stark contrast to the President's record." Jon Stewart paraphrased: "I'm going to endorse Romney because he's the Republican nominee."

909. When former Governor George Pataki endorsed Mitt Romney on Fox News, Jon Stewart pointed out it was

less than confident. Pataki began, "Now, Mitt is not a perfect candidate. He has a number of problems." Jon Stewart paused here and said, "All right! Which are very much overshadowed by his good qualities, which are...?" Pataki continued: "It's hard for blue collar families like mine to identify with him. It's hard for economic conservatives to identify with him." Stewart interrupted, "But, you know, he's good with Latinos..." to which the clip of Pataki went on to finish, "He needs to do more to reach out to Latinos."

910. Jon Stewart asks, "Can anybody offer a strong, unequivocal endorsement of Mitt Romney? Mitt Romney's wife?" The C4 Show clip that follows features Ann Romney being asked if she has to defend her husband against claims that he appears stiff, as she responds: "Well, ah, you know, I guess, I guess, we better unzip him and let the real Romney out, 'cause he is not."

911. "Now that Bush has accepted the [2004 Republican presidential] nomination, the next step, of course, is the rigging of the voting machines."

—David Letterman

912. "Tonight at the [2004] Republican National Convention, in what was called the biggest speech of his career, President Bush took on his enemy, the English language."

—Jay Leno

913. "George Bush accepted the [2004 Republican presidential] nomination and promised that if he's re-elected, he promised to start reading memos. That's a good sign."

—David Letterman

914. "Last night [at the 2004 Republican National Convention], the Republican faithful were angry. After four years of being in charge of the House, Senate, Supreme Court and Executive branch, they were not gonna take it anymore. … Yeah! Down with the people who are already down!"

   —Jon Stewart

915. "Arnold Schwarzenegger gave a terrific speech last night [at the 2004 Republican National Convention]. See, that's where the Republicans are really smart. They don't want to portray themselves as the right-wing party, so they bring in an actor to play the moderate."

   —Jay Leno

916. David Letterman on the 2004 Democrat and Republican National Conventions: "At the [Democrat] convention John Kerry showed up with all his Vietnam crewmates. And not to be outdone, next month at the Republican Convention, George W. Bush is going to show up with all his college drinking buddies."

917. "As people do better, they start voting like Republicans— unless they have too much education and vote Democratic, which proves there can be too much of a good thing."

   —Karl Rove

918. "Bush's Trillions: How to Buy the Republican Majority of Tomorrow."

   —*The New Yorker*, February 19, 2001

919. "Everyone in the blamestream media, copyright, is saying Newt Gingrich is on the ropes. Wrong, you parasites. This man will rise again, just like the sourdough he appears to be made of."

   —Stephen Colbert

920. "Newt Gingrich has a new campaign slogan: 'Now hiring!' Sixteen of Gingrich's top staff quit last week, and today, two of his top fundraisers quit. He's not even president and he's already raising the unemployment rate."

—Jay Leno

921. "Newt Gingrich is so pro-marriage, he can't stop doing it. He is so morally upright, that he's only had sex after he was married. Just not always to the woman he was married to."

—Stephen Colbert

922. "A gay activist dumped glitter all over Newt Gingrich. He wants Newt to stop being against gay marriage. But Newt believes marriage is a sacred bond between a man and his wife and his mistress and the other woman he's seeing on the side."

—Jay Leno

923. "In a new interview, Newt Gingrich says he cheated on two of his wives because he was too consumed with love for his country. Yeah, apparently he misunderstood the phrase, 'Please rise for the Pledge of Allegiance.'"

—Conan O'Brien

924. "After President Obama gave his State of the Union Address, the Republicans gave their rebuttal, during which they pointed out that Obama has repeatedly failed to solve any of the problems they created under President Bush."

—Jimmy Kimmel

925. "I will show you President Obama's birth certificate when you show me Sarah Palin's high school diploma."

—Bill Maher

926. "If conservatives get to call universal healthcare 'socialized medicine,' I get to call private, for-profit healthcare 'soulless, vampire bastards making money off human pain.'"

—Bill Maher

927. "I have a problem with people who take the Constitution loosely and the Bible literally."

—Bill Maher

928. "Of course, you call one woman you've never met a slut and a prostitute and demand that she post an internet gang-bang tape, and suddenly the lamestream media is jumping down your throat—if there were room in there with all that ham."

—Stephen Colbert, on Rush Limbaugh

929. Jon Stewart on Bush's "coalition of the willing" in the war in Iraq: "Yesterday, the president met with a group he calls the coalition of the willing. Or, as the rest of the world calls them, Britain and Spain."

930. "We have it. The smoking gun. The evidence. The potential weapon of mass destruction we have been looking for as our pretext of invading Iraq. There's just one problem—it's in North Korea."

—Jon Stewart

931. "As the Republicans continue checking underneath every available flag pin and Bible for viable candidates, presumed de facto frontrunner candidate Mitt Romney has gotta be thinking, 'What the fudge? This is starting to hurt where my feelings should be.'"

—Jon Stewart

932. "I mean Romney has been running for president since 2007. Romney's the former governor of the state where the actual Tea Party happened. He's the son of a popular Midwestern governor. He's rich. He looks like a guy you'd cast as the president in a movie. And not a movie where the president is corrupt or an asteroid is about to hit the earth, more of a light-hearted president-dad type movie. Where he commands an army but can't connect with his kids."

—Jon Stewart

933. Sarah Palin, trying to explain the midnight ride of Paul Revere: "He who warned, uh, the British that they weren't gonna be takin' away our arms, uh, by ringing those bells, and um, makin' sure as he's riding his horse through town to send those warning shots and bells that we were going to be sure and we were going to be free, and we were going to be armed."

934. Sarah Palin, apparently making an attempt at a coherent statement: "I don't know if I should Buenos Aires or Bonjour, or … this is such a melting pot. This is beautiful. I love the diversity. Yeah. There were a whole bunch of guys named Tony in the photo line, I know that."

935. Sarah Palin wrote in her book *Going Rogue*, "If God had not intended for us to eat animals, how come He made them out of meat?"

936. During an interview with Katie Couric, Sarah Palin was asked which newspapers she read. Unable to name a single paper, Palin said, "all of 'em, any of 'em."

937. "Juarez is reported to be the most dangerous city in America," said Gov. Rick Perry of Juarez, located in Mexico.

938. "The president, he put us in Libya. He is now putting us in Africa," said Michele Bachmann, apparently unaware that Libya is actually in Africa.

939. "While criticizing President Obama during an interview on 'Good Morning America' this week, Rudy Giuliani said, 'We had no domestic attacks under Bush.' You know, I knew one day we would reach a point where people would forget about 9/11, but I never thought you would be the first."

    —Seth Myers

940. Conan O'Brien said of Bachmann, "Lenscrafters is upset with Tea Partier Michele Bachmann because she called Planned Parenthood 'the Lenscrafters of abortion.' Lenscrafters released a statement today calling her 'the Costco of crazy.'"

941. Conan O'Brien said of the GOP debate, "Last night at the Republican debate MSNBC put little factoids about the candidates on the screen as they were speaking. For instance, Michele Bachmann: Pet peeve: facts. Gives Jesus the creeps. Has never seen her husband naked. Governor Rick Perry: Dumber than Bush, no lie. Motto: 'Don't mess with Texes.' In high school voted 'Most likely to execute 200+ people.' Newt Gingrich: Even fatter in real life. Carpet matches the drapes. Favorite color: Donuts."

942. "Rick Santorum has dropped out of the race. He wanted to ban gambling and outlaw pornography. And this is a guy who claims Romney is out of touch with America."

    —David Letterman

943. "Newt Gingrich wants to repeal child labor laws. Ladies and gentlemen, this is the man that we need to lead us into the 18th century."

　　　　　　　　　　　　　　　　　　—David Letterman

944. "Republicans are having trouble luring Gov. Chris Christie into the presidential race. They should try pie."

　　　　—David Letterman, on the New Jersey Governor

945. Of Gingrich's campaign, Jay Leno said, "Newt Gingrich has a new campaign slogan: 'Now hiring!' Sixteen of Gingrich's top staff quit last week, and today, two of his top fundraisers quit. He's not even president and he's already raising the unemployment rate."

946. "He believes that the tax should be flat just like the Earth."

　　　　　　　　　　　　　　—Jay Leno, on Rick Perry

947. "Protecting young girls from cervical cancer? Rick Perry left himself vulnerable to charges of having a tiny speck of humanity, which is very bad for a Republican candidate. So he announced a new policy for Texas. For every child who gets the HPV vaccine, he will execute two Mexicans."

　　　　　　　　　　　　　　　　　　—Bill Maher

948. "If you're keeping score at home, they have now applauded executions at the Republican debate, they have cheered letting an uninsured man die, and they booed an active duty U.S. serviceman for being gay. I don't know how you get to the right with this crowd but Ron Paul's new campaign ad is just the Rodney King beating to the sound of children laughing."

　　　　　　　　　　　　　　—Bill Maher, on the GOP

949. Of the current Republican personalities, Bill Maher noted, "If Bachmann and Palin get in, that's two bimbos. And there there's Mitt Romney, the millionaire and Newt Gingrich, a professor. We just need a skipper and a buddy and we've got 'Gilligan's Island.'"

950. Regarding the corrupt status of the GOP today, Bill Maher said, "Rick Perry said, 'I only took $5,000 from Merck. Are you saying I can be bought for $5,000? I'm offended.' This is how degraded our politics are. How dare you call me a cheap whore. I will have you know I'm a high-priced whore."

951. "Apparently, Mitt Romney is planning to build a huge addition onto his beach house in California. And here's the cool part: They're using the same wood that they used to build Mitt Romney."
    —Jimmy Fallon, on the GOP presidential candidate

952. "More and more information coming out about our other presidential candidates. Like, did you know that Mitt Romney's real name is Willard? He was born Willard. Well, thank god he had the good sense to change it to 'Mitt.' That's so much more accessible than Will,"
    —Jay Leno, on the GOP candidate.

953. "Mitt Romney was on the 'Today Show' and admitted he likes to read the 'Twilight' books and watch 'American Idol.' If elected, he would be the 1st Mormon and the 1st 13-year-old girl to be President."
    —Jimmy Kimmel, on the likely GOP presidential candidate

954. A recent study by Center for Media and Public Affairs (CMPA) found that in 2011 the jokes on late night

comedy/talk shows targeted Republicans more than Democrats, proving how difficult it is to take many Republican politicians and policies seriously. CMPA President Dr. Robert Lichter commented on the disparity: "This shows that it's hard to vote for somebody while you're laughing at them."

955. Rex Rammell, a Republican from Idaho, once joked to a crowd of hunters during his failed 2009 Gubernatorial campaign that one could purchase licenses to hunt President Obama: "Obama tags."

956. Former Republican presidential candidate Herman Cain joked that he would erect an insurmountable electric fence to electrify and kill those that attempt to enter the country illegally. Government sanctioned electrocution has been outdated for some time in this country and has never been a joke.

957. "Carbon dioxide is portrayed as harmful. But there isn't even one study that can be produced that shows that carbon dioxide is a harmful gas."
—Michele Bachmann, 2009

958. "Dick Cheney said he felt terrible about shooting a 78-year-old man, but on the bright side, it did give him a great idea about how to fix Social Security."
—Bill Maher

959. "To the vice president's credit, he did own up to it. On FOX News he said the fault was his, he can't blame anybody else. Boy, it's amazing, the only time you get accountability out of this administration is when they are actually holding a smoking gun."
—Bill Maher, on Dick Cheney's shooting of an elderly man

960. "Speaker John Boehner complained that Obama ordered the U.S. military into combat in Libya without clearly defining the mission to the American people and Congress. See, apparently, you're only allowed to do that when invading Iraq."

—Jay Leno

961. "In his first speech as Speaker, Boehner thanked his loved ones—tobacco lobbyists, the oil companies, the CEOs."

—Jay Leno

962. "The Supreme Court is deciding right now whether the government can mandate that all Americans buy health insurance. Rick Santorum said, 'There's no way I'm letting the government make me go on a man date.'"

—Conan O'Brien

963. "A recent survey showed that Rick Santorum is the favorite GOP candidate among Republican women. When he heard that, Santorum was like, 'Wait—women have the right to vote?'"

—Jimmy Fallon

964. "Rumors now that Mitt Romney might pick Rick Santorum for his VP running mate. But Rick is dubious. He thinks two guys on the same ticket might be gay."

—David Letterman

965. "Sarah Palin's book is number one on Amazon.com right now. Stephen King actually has the number two book. Very scary new book called 'Sarah Palin Becomes President.'"

—Jimmy Kimmel

966. "Michele Bachmann says she will launch her presidential campaign in either Massachusetts or New Hampshire as soon as she figures out which is which. There could be some eligibility problems for her. She has her birth certificate, but nobody can produce her high school diploma."

—Jay Leno

967. "In a speech in Canada, former President George W. Bush said he was proud that when he was in office he didn't sell his soul, which is true. He rented it to Dick Cheney, who then sublet it to Halliburton, but it's totally different."

—Jay Leno

968. How many Republicans does it take to screw in a light bulb? None. If the liberals would just leave it alone, it would change itself.

969. Two wealthy Repubs are sitting in a restaurant, one of them being the owner. The owner turns to his guest and says, "See? I'm doing my part to help the economy, I just opened up three new jobs in my restaurant." Just as the two get finished toasting each other's success, the busboy comes by to clear off their dishes and says, "I know, I have all three of them."

970. Two guys are sitting around talking about politics. One of them asks the other, "So why are you a Democrat?" "Because my daddy and granddaddy were Democrats," was the man's reply. "What if your daddy and granddaddy were horse thieves?" "In that case, I guess I'd be a Republican."

971. Virginia State Rep. Dave Albo, after promoting a bill for mandatory transvaginal probing of women who sought abortions, joked about his wife refusing his sexual advances. His lack of understanding of basically state sponsored rape prevented him from seeing that his wife was not laughing.

972. "The founder of Home Depot announced that he is supporting Mitt Romney for president. It's kind of a nice story, because Mitt Romney was actually assembled with parts from Home Depot."

—Jimmy Fallon

973. "The new season of 'Lost' kicked off tonight. If you haven't seen it, 'Lost' is about a group of desperate people out of touch with the world. It's based on the true story of the Republican Party."

—Craig Ferguson

974. "Senator Larry Craig asked the court on Wednesday to void the guilty plea he made, following his arrest last year in a bathroom sex sting operation. Then, when the request was denied, he asked if he could use the bathroom."

—Amy Poehler

975. "Thirty-eight million people watched Barack Obama at the stadium in Denver. There were 84,000 full-throated supporters who turned out there at the field. The Republicans fired back today. They say, 'We can also fill a stadium with thousands of screaming people. For example, the Superdome during Hurricane Katrina.'"

—Bill Maher

976. "The Republicans, who had 3 candidates who proudly said they did not believe in Evolution … which became ironic when their campaigns quickly died off in favor of stronger, fitter campaigns."

—Bill Maher

977. Former GOP Presidential hopeful Herman Cain urged Americans to reread the Constitution, particularly the part regarding "life, liberty, and the pursuit of happiness." As it turns out, that famous phrase is not found in the Constitution, but does feature rather prominently in the Declaration of Independence.

978. Former Tea Party candidate Christine O'Donnell, like many Republicans, appears to be confused by science. On the O'Reilly factor, she said, "American scientific companies are cross-breeding humans and animals and coming up with mice with fully functioning human brains."

979. Proving yet again that basic science eludes her, Christine O'Donnell said that if evolution is a fact, "why aren't monkeys still evolving into humans?"

980. "Now there's a problem with the paperwork with Dick Cheney's heart operation. The insurance company doesn't want to pay. They said for Cheney being heartless was a pre-existing condition."

—Jay Leno, on the former vice president

981. "Rick Santorum has now said if elected President, he would ban hardcore pornography. Which is why Mitt Romney changed his slogan, 'Mitt Romney: Because Santorum Would Ban Hard Core Pornography.'"

—Conan O'Brien

982. "You know who Boehner is, right? He's that orange looking guy. See, for Republicans that counts as diversity."

—Jay Leno, on the house speaker

983. "And make no mistake, Mitt Romney's a rich guy. He is so rich, even his illegal immigrants have illegal immigrants working for them. That's how rich. He is so rich, the last time he went hunting; he shot Dick Cheney in the face. Okay, that is rich. He is so rich, in his fantasy football league, he drafts owners. That's how rich."

—Jay Leno, on Mitt Romney

984. "They always throw around this term 'the liberal elite.' And I kept thinking to myself about the Christian right. What's more elite than believing that only you will go to heaven?"

—Jon Stewart, on the Christian conservatives dominating the Republican party

985. "And more and more Republicans are calling on Newt Gingrich to drop out of the campaign. Well, I don't want the say things look bad for Newt, but his ex-wives now are starting to outnumber his supporters. Okay, that's never a good sign. Never a good sign."

—Jay Leno

986. "text too tighton with the Wisconsin primary. Wisconsin Democrats are accusing Mitt Romney of handing out free sub sandwiches in exchange for votes. Which explains why Newt Gingrich today voted for Mitt Romney. Seven times."

—Conan O'Brien

987. "Oh, I saw the worst reality show last night. Have you seen this one? It's called 'The Republican Debate.' Anybody watch that? It was on CNN. You know who the big winner was? 'American Idol' on Fox."

—Jay Leno

988. "Puerto Rico is a territory of the United States. And yesterday, Santorum greeted the locals by telling them if Puerto Rico wants to become a state, they need to start speaking English. Like Jesus does. Only Rick Santorum would go to someone's native land and tell them they're speaking the wrong language. And then he told them to stop being so Mexican. He's got a shot to be our funniest President ever."

—Jimmy Kimmel, on Rick Santorum

989. "This week in Ohio, Mitt Romney has been trying to present himself as a blue collar candidate. Did you hear that? He's trying to connect with regular folk. Unfortunately, it doesn't help that his opening line is, 'Hello, my fellow peasants.'"

—Conan O'Brien, on the millionaire Republican candidate

990. "I read today, the earth's population is now well past seven billion people … seven billion. And still, the Republicans can't find one candidate they really like."

—Jay Leno, on the GOP presidential candidates

991. "In the United States there are nearly 1.8 million dead people who are still registered to vote. Yeah. Dead people are still registered to vote. Yeah. As a matter of fact, they're the group that's most passionate about Mitt Romney."

—Conan O'Brien

992. "Rick Santorum said this week he wants to restore religious values to government. You know, like they do in Iran."
—Jay Leno, on the former GOP presidential hopeful

993. "Mitt Romney said this week if he's elected, he won't let Iran get nuclear weapons. Other Republicans were quick to respond. Newt Gingrich said it would be impossible to enforce. Ron Paul said it's none of our business. And Rick Perry said—[blank stare]"
—Craig Ferguson

994. "Herman was unaware that China is a nuclear power. He didn't know that China is a nuclear power. Been that way since 1964, had no idea China was a nuclear power. And I said to myself, 'Hey, Herman, how about making an unwanted advance on a history book?'"
—David Letterman

995. "The Republican War on Women is a liberal invention, like global warming and the female orgasm. Where's the evidence?".
—Stephen Colbert

996. "Studies are showing that Republican candidates are buying a lot of their ad time on the Weather Channel. Yeah. You can tell because last night the weatherman blamed the cold front on immigration and gay marriage."
—Conan O'Brien

997. "Believe me, whatever you think, Mitt Romney, this guy is smart with money. He knows how to make money. In fact, turns out, he's had at least 11 money funds and partnerships in low tax foreign countries like Bermuda, the Cayman Islands, Switzerland, even Luxembourg. You

know what that means? His money has had more foreign policy experience than he has."

—Jay Leno, on Mitt Romney

998. "Newt Gingrich was cheating on his second wife while he was prosecuting Bill Clinton for the Monica Lewinsky thing. In other words, Newt puts the 'hippo' in 'Hypocrite.'"

—Jimmy Kimmel

999. "Mitt Romney celebrated his 65th birthday today. They had to be very careful lighting all those candles around so much hair product. But there were no incidents."
—Jimmy Kimmel, on the well-coiffed GOP candidate

1,000. "John Boehner will be the new speaker unless, out of habit, he blocks his own confirmation."

—Stephen Colbert, on the Speaker of the House

1,001. "It's interesting what former presidents do when they leave office. Bush is now working as a motivational speaker. And if you want to be motivated, who better to turn to than the guy who invaded the wrong country and started a depression."

—David Letterman, on former President Bush

Conclusion

If you've made it this far (and we hope that you have), then you've just read 1,001 different ways that the Republican Party is trying (and succeeding) to screw the middle class. None of this information was made up, and we checked all of our sources twice (like Santa!). The scary thing is, if this book was titled *2,002 Ways the Republican Party is Screwing the Middle Class*, we could have done it!

The point of us at PRD deciding to write this book was the hope that maybe the people who aren't aware of the detrimental ways in which the Republican Party is acting towards the middle class would be able to see first-hand over one thousand different examples. We want the majority to hold the power over the power elite, because if we all unite together, we can overpower them. (We certainly cannot outspend them!)

While they may have had a different upbringing than most of us, it does not mean that they should act better than us. We are the ones who hold the power to elect them, and if this is how they will continue to treat us, we should go out to the polls and vote against them. People consistently forget how much power they hold. With everything that you've read in this book, it should set off a light bulb in your brain that these people don't care about you. If they don't care about you, don't vote for them. We have the power, and if we don't use it, then we will end up suffering the consequences.

Now this is anything but a threat. It is a call to action. No longer should we stand for those who have ulterior motives force us to do things that we are morally against or continue to hurt us financially. The freedoms that we are trying to hold onto are being tugged away by these Republicans, and if we let go, then we will never see them back again. This is still the land of the free, and we must stand up and make sure that it continues to be. We at the PRD hope that everyone who picked up this book has learned something, and that by us working together, we can continue to improve our democracy, rather than letting the power elite weaken it.

Source List

1. www.alternet.org
2. www.cnn.com
3. www.nymag.com
4. www.politico.com
5. www.greedyrepublicans.com
6. www.democrats.org
7. www.businessweek.com; www.huffingtonpost.com
8. www.washingtonpost.com
9. www.democrats.org
10. Ibid.
11. Ibid.
12. www.sacramento.cbslocal.com
13. www.democrats.org
14. Ibid.
15. www.abcnews.com
16. www.democrats.org
17. Ibid.
18. Ibid.
19. www.nytimes.com
20. www.democrats.org
21. Ibid.
22. Ibid.
23. Ibid.
24. Ibid.
25. Ibid.
26. Ibid.
27. www.nytimes.com
28. www.businessweek.com
29. www.democrats.org
30. www.npr.org
31. www.opensecrets.org
32. Ibid.
33. www.opensecrets.org
34. www.democrats.org
35. www.addictinginfo.org
36. www.cbpp.org
37. www.keepinggophonest.com
38. Ibid.
39. Ibid.
40. www.huffingtonpost.com
41. www.businessweek.com
42. www.mittismean.org
43. www.nytimes.com; www.mittismean.org
44. www.mittismean.org
45. www.newyorker.com
46. www.wallstreetjournal.com
47. www.politicalcorrection.org
48. www.addictinginfo.org
49. Ibid.
50. www.huffingtonpost.com
51. www.democrats.org
52. www.opensecrets.org

53. www.motherjones.com
54. Ibid.
55. www.buzzfeed.com
56. www.mediaite.com
57. www.democrats.org
58. www.addictinginfo.org
59. www.thinkprogress.org
60. Ibid.
61. Ibid.
62. www.opensecrets.org
63. www.washingtonpost.com
64. www.opensecrets.com
65. Ibid.
66. www.democrats.org
67. Ibid.
68. www.motherjones.com
69. www.thebottom99percent.com
70. www.wikiquote.org
71. Ibid.
72. Ibid.
73. Ibid.
74. Ibid.
75. www.cnn.com
76. Ibid.
77. Ibid.
78. www.mediamatters.org
79. www.thinkprogress.org
80. www.mediamatters.org
81. www.wikiquote.org
82. www.newyorker.com
83. *Naked Republicans,* Shelley Lewis, Villard Books, 2006
84. www.indecisionforever.com
85. www.motherjones.com
86. Ibid.
87. Ibid.
88. Ibid.
89. Ibid.
90. www.asr.com; www.motherjones.com
91. www.motherjones.com
92. Ibid.
93. www.politico.com
94. Ibid.
95. www.progressillinois.com
96. www.thestar.com
97. www.ucsusa.org
98. www.huffingtonpost.com
99. Ibid.
100. Ibid.
101. www.coloradoindependent.com
102. Ibid.
103. Ibid.
104. Ibid.
105. Ibid.
106. Ibid.
107. www.thinkprogress.com
108. Ibid.
109. Ibid.
110. Ibid.
111. Ibid.
112. www.nytimes.com
113. Ibid.
114. www.washingtonpost.com
115. Ibid.
116. Ibid.
117. Ibid.

118. www.dailykos.com
119. www.mediamatters.com
120. Ibid.
121. Ibid.
122. www.npr.org
123. Ibid.
124. Ibid.
125. Ibid.
126. www.tpmlivewire.com
127. www.washingtonpost.com; www.slate.com
128. www.nytimes.com; www.slate.com
129. www.conservapedia.com
130. www.thinkprogress.org
131. www.democrats.org
132. Ibid.
133. www.motherjones.com
134. www.politicsdaily.com
135. www.ctj.org
136. www.washingtonpost.com
137. www.politifact.com
138. www.latimes.com
139. www.democrats.org
140. Ibid.
141. Ibid.
142. Ibid.
143. www.nytimes.com
144. www.democrats.com
145. www.crooksandilars.com
146. www.motherjones.com
147. www.gnelson.com
148. www.commondreams.com
149. Ibid.
150. Ibid.
151. www.motherjones.com
152. Ibid.
153. www.thinkprogress.com
154. Ibid.
155. www.republicandirtytricks.com
156. www.perrspectives.com
157. www.motherjones.com
158. www.slate.com
159. www.nymag.com
160. www.addictinginfo.org
161. www.keepinggophonest.com
162. Ibid.
163. www.motherjones.com
164. www.motherjones.com; www.omaha.com
165. www.motherjones.com
166. Ibid.
167. www.huffingtonpost.com
168. www.huffingtonpost.com
169. www.rhrealitycheck.org
170. www.washingtonpost.com
171. www.thinkprogress.com
172. www.baloon-juice.com
173. www.tpmdc.com
174. www.wired.com; www.msnbc.com; www.slate.com

175. www.brennancenter.org
176. www.ohiohistorycentral.org
177. www.americanhistory.com
178. www.americanpresidents.org
179. www.republicanoffenders.com
180. Ibid.
181. www.thinkprogress.org
182. www.pbs.org
183. Ibid.
184. Ibid.
185. www.extremelysmart.com
186. Ibid.
187. Ibid.
188. www.upenn.edu
189. www.usnews.com
190. www.cbsnews.com
191. www.seattletimes.com
192. www.watergate.info
193. www.crooksandliars.com
194. www.infoplease.com
195. www.gopdirtytricks.com
196. www.washingtonmonthly.com
197. www.gopdirtytricks.com; www.consortiumnews.com
198. www.gopdirtytricks.com
199. www.theatlantic.com
200. www.gopdirtytricks.com
201. www.reclaimdemocracy.org
202. www.gopdirtytricks.com
203. www.watergate.info
204. www.guardian.co.uk
205. www.abcnews.com
206. www.cnn.com; www.washingtonpost.com; www.dailykos.com; www.dkosopedia.com
207. *185 Stupid Things Republicans Have Said,* Ted Reuter, Andrews McMeel, 2008
208. *Stupid White Men—and Other Sorry Excuses for the State of the Nation!,* Michael Moore, HarperCollins, 2004
209. www.thinkprogress.org
210. www.pbs.org
211. *Lies and the Lying Liars Who Tell Them,* Al Franken, Dutton, 2003
212. *185 Stupid Things Republicans Have Said,* Ted Reuter, Andrews McMeel, 2008
213. *Naked Republicans,* Shelley Lewis, Villard Books, 2006
214. www.nytimes.com
215. www.washingtonpost.com

216. www.washingtonpost.
     com; www.slate.com
217. www.wired.com;
     www.washingtonpost.
     com;
     www.slate.com
218. www.times.com
219. www.latimes.com
220. www.b.3cdn.net
221. www.dailybulletin.
     com; www.b.3cdn.net
222. www.addictinginfo.org
223. www.democrats.com
224. www.nationalpost.com
225. www.michaelmoore.
     com
226. www.pbs.org
227. www.miamiherald.com
228. www.thinkprogress.
     com
229. www.issues2000.org
230. www.thinkprogress.
     org
231. www.pbs.org
232. www.nytimes.com
233. www.mediamatters.org
234. www.salon.com
235. www.freerepublic.com
236. www.salon.com; www.
     presidentialufo.com
237. www.philly.com
238. www.democratichub.
     com
239. www.theatlantic.com
240. www.legal-dictionary.
     com
241. www.commondreams.
     org

242. www.nytimes.com
243. www.bloomberg.com
244. www.newsdesk.org
245. www.californiachroni-
     cle.com
246. www.telegraph.co.uk
247. www.reuter.com
248. www.telegraph.co.uk
249. Ibid.
250. www.thebottom99per-
     cent.com
251. www.wsj.com
252. www.time.com
253. Ibid.
254. Ibid.
255. www.opensecrets.org
256. www.commondreams.
     org; www.slate.com
257. www.cbsnews.com;
     www.latimes.com;
     www.slate.com
258. www.washingtonpost.
     com; www.slate.com
259. www.nytimes.com;
     www.slate.com
260. www.washingtonpost.
     com; www.slate.com
261. www.usatoday.com;
     www.slate.com
262. www.washingtonpost.
     com; www.slate.com
263. www.salon.com; www.
     slate.com
264. www.freerepublic.com;
     www.washingtonpost.
     com; www.slate.com
265. www.prwatch.com;
     www.slate.com

266. www.sourcewatch.org;
www.slate.com
267. www.cnn.com;
www.slate.com
268. www.washington-
times.com;
www.slate.com
269. www.slate.com
270. www.democratichub.
com
271. www.cnn.com
272. www.democratichub.
com
273. www.salon.com;
www.baltimorechroni-
cle.com; www.bbc.
co.uk; www.b.3cdn.net
274. www.b.3cdn.net; www.
talkingpointsmemo.
com
275. www.washingtonpost.
com
276. www.globalissues.org;
www.dailynews.com
277. www.globalissues.org;
www.truthout.org
278. Ibid.
279. Ibid.
280. www.thedailybeast.com
281. www.politico.com
282. www.thehill.com
283. www.leisureguy.com
284. www.awolbush.com;
www.huffingtonpost.
com
285. www.awolbush.com
286. www.politifact.com
287. www.wsj.com

288. www.foreignpolicy.com
289. www.nytimes.com
290. www.worldcantwait.
net
291. www.washingtonpost.
com
292. Ibid.
293. www.cnn.com
294. www.nytimes.com
295. www.politico.com
296. www.amnestyusa.org
297. www.cryptome.org;
www.wsj.com; www.
alternet.org
298. www.fff.org
299. www.politico.com
300. Ibid.
301. Ibid.
302. www.thinkprogress.
com
303. Ibid.
304. www.weeklystandard.
com
305. www.foreign.senate.gov
306. Ibid.
307. www.nytimes.com
308. www.thinkprogress.
com
309. www.gnelson.com
310. www.time.com
311. www.washingtonpost.
com
312. Ibid.
313. www.commondreams.
org
314. Ibid.
315. www.telegraph.co.uk
316. www.bcc.co.uk

317. www.telegraph.co.uk
318. Ibid.
319. www.washingtonpost.com
320. www.mediamatters.org
321. www.volokh.com
322. www.washington-monthly.com
323. www.crooksandliars.com
324. www.commondreams.org
325. www.foxnews.com
326. Ibid.
327. www.motherjones.com
328. Ibid.
329. www.usliberals.com
330. www.msnbc.com
331. www.time.com
332. www.nytimes.com
333. www.usliberals.com
334. Ibid.
335. www.crooksandliars.com
336. Ibid.
337. Ibid.
338. www.slate.com
339. www.washingtonpost.com; www.slate.com
340. www.nytimes.com; www.slate.com
341. www.politifact.com; www.washingtonpost.com; www.slate.com
342. www.theatlantic.com
343. www.thinkprogress.com
344. www.economist.com; www.hoover.org
345. www.critics.org; www.baremetal.com
346. www.criticism.com
347. Ibid.
348. www.criticism.com; www.wsws.org
349. www.nytimes.com
350. www.critics.org
351. www.criticism.com; www.opposingviews.com
352. www.drugpolicty.org
353. Ibid.
354. www.drugpolicy.org; www.drugwarfacts.org
355. Ibid.
356. www.unitedliberty.org
357. www.chippewa.com
358. www.forbes.com
359. www.thehill.com
360. www.thinkprogress.com
361. www.opensecrets.org
362. www.nytimes.com
363. www.priceofoil.org
364. www.huffingtonpost.com
365. www.dailykos.com
366. www.thinkprogress.com; www.forbes.com
367. www.iwatchnews.org
368. www.ucsusa.org
369. www.thinkprogress.org
370. www.latimes.com

371. www.dirtyenergymoney.com
372. www.addictinginfo.org
373. Ibid.
374. www.politico.com; www.salon.com
375. www.salon.com
376. Ibid.
377. Ibid.
378. www.salon.com; www.thinkprogress.com
379. www.salon.com
380. www.washingtonpost.com
381. Ibid.
382. www.politico.com
383. Ibid.
384. www.democrats.org
385. www.excite.com
386. www.rightwingwatch.org
387. www.msnbc.com; www.nytimes.com; www.boston.com; www.slate.com
388. www.washingtonpost.com; www.slate.com
389. Ibid.
390. www.citizensforethics.org
391. www.slate.com
392. www.washingtonpost.com; www.slate.com
393. www.democrats.com
394. www.washingtonpost.com
395. www.nytimes.com
396. Ibid.
397. Ibid.
398. www.thenations.com
399. Ibid.
400. Ibid.
401. Ibid.
402. Ibid.
403. www.dirtyenergymoney.com
404. Ibid.
405. www.ucsusa.com
406. Ibid.
407. www.cbsnews.com
408. Ibid.
409. Ibid.
410. www.politico.com
411. Ibid.
412. www.inhofe.senate.gov
413. www.dirtyenergymoney.com
414. www.climatescience-watch.org
415. www.guardian.co.uk
416. Ibid.
417. www.opensecrets.com
418. www.nytimes.com
419. www.abcnews.com
420. Ibid.
421. www.npr.org
422. www.abcnews.com
423. ww.npr.gov
424. www.abcnews.com
425. Ibid.
426. Ibid.
427. Ibid.
428. www.opensecrets.org
429. www.abcnews.com

430. www.washingtonpost.com
431. Ibid.
432. www.opensecrets.org
433. Ibid.
434. www.truthdig.com
435. www.businessweek.com
436. www.scotusblog.com
437. www.priceofoil.org
438. www.commondreams.org
439. Ibid.
440. Ibid.
441. www.guardian.co.uk
442. www.prwatch.org; www.slate.com
443. www.washingtonpost.com
444. www.twincities.com
445. www.thinkprogress.com; www.aikenstandard.com
446. www.politico.com; www.b.3cdn.net
447. Ibid.
448. Ibid.
449. www.b.3cdn.net; www.tampabay.com; www.politico.com; www.citizensforethics.org; www.miamiherald.com
450. www.politico.com; www.b.3cdn.net
451. www.mcclatchydc.com; www.b.3cdn.net
452. www.knoxnews.com; www.b.3cdn.net
453. www.huffingtonpost.com
454. www.crewmostcorrupt.org; www.b.3cdn.net
455. www.washingtonpost.com
456. www.conservapedia.com
457. www.rightwingwatch.org
458. www.guardian.co.uk
459. www.crooksandliars.com
460. www.politicalcorrection.org
461. www.thenation.com
462. www.politifact.com
463. www.thenation.com
464. Ibid.
465. Ibid.
466. Ibid.
467. www.michiganbuildingtrades.org
468. www.thenation.com
469. Ibid.
470. www.concordmonitor.com
471. Ibid.
472. www.reagan.procon.org
473. www.tnr.com
474. www.latimes.com
475. www.nhinsider.com
476. www.huffingtonpost.com

477. www.sun-sentinel.com; www.thinkprogress.com
478. www.reasonablegovt.com
479. www.buffalonews.com
480. www.salon.com
481. www.washingtonpost.com
482. www.offthecharts.org; www.cnn.com
483. www.keepinggophonest.com; www.wrko.com
484. www.keepinggophonest.com; www.msnbc.com
485. www.keepinggophonest.com
486. www.keepinggophonest.com; www.boston.com; www.msnbc.com
487. www.politicalcorrection.com
488. Ibid.
489. www.huffingtonpost.com
490. www.sunjournal.com
491. www.thinkprogress.org
492. www.huffingtonpost.com
493. www.dailyfinance.com
494. Ibid.
495. www.huffingtonpost.com; www.bangordailynews.com
496. www.alternet.org
497. Ibid.
498. Ibid.
499. Ibid.
500. www.thebottom99percent.com; www.alternet.org
501. www.ontheissues.org
502. www.ncpolicywatch.org
503. www.democrats.org
504. www.abcnews.com
505. www.thinkprogress.org
506. www.politicalcorrection.org
507. www.thinkprogress.org
508. Ibid.
509. www.politicalcorrection.org
510. www.cnn.com
511. Ibid.
512. www.nytimes.com
513. Ibid.
514. www.thinkprogress.com
515. www.democrats.org
516. www.thinkprogress.org
517. www.cnn.com
518. www.digg.com
519. Ibid.
520. www.mlive.com
521. www.rootsaction.org
522. Ibid.
523. Ibid.
524. www.democrats.org
525. www.nytimes.com
526. www.rollingstones.com
527. www.thehill.com
528. www.thinkprogress.com
529. www.cnn.com

530. Ibid.
531. Ibid.
532. Ibid.
533. www.politicalcorrection.org
534. www.rightwingwatch.org
535. www.npr.org
536. www.thinkprogress.org
537. www.nytimes.com
538. www.politifact.com
539. www.democrats.senate.gov
540. www.minnesota.publicradio.org
541. www.missourijournal.com
542. www.fff.org
543. Ibid.
544. Ibid.
545. www.masslive.com
546. www.knoxnews.com; www.b.3cdn.net
547. www.b.3cdn.net; www.latimes.com
548. www.huffingtonpost.com
549. www.democrats.budget.house.gov
550. Ibid.
551. Ibid.
552. Ibid.
553. www.ctj.org
554. Ibid.
555. Ibid.
556. Ibid.
557. www.thinkprogress.org
558. www.ctj.org
559. www.postandcourier.com
560. www.cbsnews.com
561. www.thinkprogress.com
562. www.news.cincinnati.com
563. www.businessweek.com; www.thinkprogress.com
564. www.thinkprogress.com
565. Ibid.
566. www.thinkprogress.org; www.wsj.com
567. www.jsonline.com
568. www.thinkprogress.org
569. Ibid.
570. Ibid.
571. www.ktar.com; www.thinkprogress.org
572. www.thinkprogress.org
573. www.americanprogress.org
574. Ibid.
575. Ibid.
576. Ibid.
577. www.dailykos.com
578. www.taxpolicycenter.org
579. www.commondreams.org
580. www.dailykos.com
581. www.taxpolicycenter.com
582. Ibid.
583. Ibid.

584. Ibid.
585. www.politicalcorrection.org
586. Azcentral.com
587. www.slate.com
588. www.campaign2012.newamerica.net
589. www.nytimes.com
590. www.talkingpointsmemo.com
591. www.epi.org
592. www.taxpolicycenter.org
593. Ibid.
594. Ibid.
595. Ibid.
596. Ibid.
597. Ibid.
598. Ibid.
599. Ibid.
600. Ibid.
601. Ibid.
602. Ibid.
603. www.alternet.org
604. www.taxpolicycenter.org
605. Ibid.
606. www.nytimes.com
607. www.huffingtonpost.com
608. www.milhs.org; www.cbpp.org
609. www.thinkprogress.org
610. www.commondreams.org
611. www.thinkprogress.org; www.politico.com; www.thehill.com
612. www.nytimes.com
613. No Citation
614. www.nytimes.com
615. www.thinkprogress.com
616. www.thebottom99percent.com
617. www.motherjones.com
618. www.democrats.org
619. www.motherjones.com
620. www.rightwingwatch.org
621. Ibid.
622. Ibid.
623. www.thinkprogress.org
624. www.nytimes.com
625. Ibid.
626. Ibid.
627. www.brainyquote.com
628. www.addictinginfo.com
629. Ibid.
630. Ibid.
631. www.alternet.org
632. www.wsj.com; www.alternet.org
633. www.washingtonmonthly.com; www.motherjones.com
634. www.washingtonpost.com
635. www.msnbc.com
636. www.addictinginfo.org
637. Ibid.
638. www.motherjones.com
639. www.thinkprogress.com

640. www.thinkprogress.com; www.ontheissues.org
641. www.foxnews.com
642. www.ontheissues.org
643. Ibid.
644. www.motherjones.com
645. Ibid.
646. Ibid.
647. Ibid.
648. www.time.com
649. www.thinkprogress.org
650. www.motherjones.com
651. Ibid.
652. www.forbes.com
653. www.thinkprogress.com
654. Ibid.
655. www.thenation.com
656. www.thinkprogress.com
657. *Why I Hate Republicans*, Randy Howe, Lyons Press, 2004
658. www.huffingtonpost.com
659. Ibid.
660. www.buzzfeed.com
661. www.pressherald.com
662. www.azcapitoltimes.com
663. www.candiesfoundation.org
664. www.chicagoist.com
665. www.postcrescent.com
666. www.chicagoist.com
667. www.pol.moveon.org
668. www.motherjones.com
669. www.talkingpointsmemo.com
670. Ibid.
671. Ibid.
672. www.nytimes.com
673. www.thinkprogress.com
674. www.conservapedia.com
675. www.keepinggophonest.com
676. www.thinkprogress.com
677. Ibid.
678. www.politifact.com
679. www.thenation.com
680. www.rightwingwatch.org
681. Ibid.
682. www.politifact.com
683. www.time.com
684. www.newyorker.com
685. Ibid.
686. www.mediamatters.com
687. www.republicansagainst8.com
688. www.mediamatters.org
689. www.goodasyou.org
690. www.politicalcorrection.org
691. www.thinkprogress.org
692. Ibid.
693. www.huffingtonpost.com
694. Ibid.
695. Ibid.
696. www.politico.com
697. www.metroweekly.com
698. Ibid.

699. www.dailycaller.com
700. www.addictinginfo.org
701. Ibid.
702. www.wnd.com
703. www.americansfor-truth.com
704. www.cwfa.org
705. www.huffingtonpost.com
706. www.theatlantic.com
707. www.addictinginfo.com
708. Ibid.
709. Ibid.
710. Ibid.
711. Ibid.
712. Ibid.
713. Ibid.
714. Ibid.
715. www.talkingpoints-memo.com
716. Ibid.
717. Ibid.
718. Ibid.
719. Ibid.
720. www.ctj.org
721. Ibid.
722. www.theatlantic.com
723. www.post-gazette.com
724. www.eia.gov
725. www.abcnews.com
726. Ibid.
727. www.politifact.com
728. www.abcnews.com
729. www.politicalcorrec-tion.org
730. Ibid.
731. Ibid.
732. Ibid.
733. www.gopdirtytricks.com
734. Ibid.
735. www.washingtonpost.com
736. www.gopdirtytricks.com
737. Ibid.
738. www.motherjones.com
739. www.huffingtonpost.com
740. www.latenightparents.com
741. www.conservapedia.com
742. www.additinginfo.com
743. www.crooksandliars.com
744. www.perrspectives.com
745. www.cbpp.org
746. www.addictinginfo.org
747. www.abcnews.com
748. www.mediamatters.org
749. www.motherjones.com
750. www.nymag.com
751. www.politifact.com
752. Ibid.
753. Ibid.
754. Ibid.
755. Ibid.
756. www.conservapedia.com
757. www.prospect.org
758. www.attackwatch.com;
www.msnbc.com

759. www.conservapedia.com
760. www.washingtonpost.com
761. www.nytimes.com
762. Ibid.
763. Ibid.
764. www.motherjones.com
765. Ibid.
766. www.realclearpolitics.com
767. www.people-press.org
768. www.publicpolicypolling.com
769. www.nytimes.com
770. www.motherjones.com
771. www.wsj.com; www.motherjones.com
772. www.msnbc.com
773. www.thenation.com
774. www.politifact.com
775. www.politico.com
776. www.westmoreland.house.gov
777. www.politifact.com
778. www.thinkprogress.com
779. www.cnn.com; www.americablog.com
780. www.thinkprogress.com
781. www.cbo.gov; www.thinkprogress.org
782. www.thinkprogress.org
783. www.politicalcorrection.org
784. www.motherjones.com; www.politifact.com
785. www.washingtonpost.com
786. www.thinkprogress.org
787. www.motherjones.com;www.conservapedia.com
788. www.politifact.com
789. www.huffingtonpost.com
790. www.coloradoindependent.com
791. www.cnn.com; www.politicalcorrection.org
792. www.motherjones.com
793. www.huffingtonpost.com
794. www.politico.com; www.b.3cdn.net
795. www.keepinggophonest.com; www.nytimes.com
796. www.democrats.org
797. www.angryblacklady.com
798. www.nytimes.com
799. www.angryblacklady.com
800. www.cnn.com
801. www.huffingtonpost.com
802. www.notable-quotes.com
803. Ibid.
804. Ibid.
805. www.newyorker.com
806. www.wikiquote.org
807. www.mlive.com
808. www.opensecrets.org

809. www.thehill.com
810. www.mlive.com
811. www.motherjones.com
812. www.mlive.com
813. www.democrats.org
814. www.washingtonpost.com
815. www.nymag.com
816. www.motherjones.com
817. www.nytimes.com
818. Ibid.
819. www.motherjones.com
820. www.nytimes.com
821. www.democrats.org
822. www.washingtonpost.com
823. www.crooksandliars.com
824. www.vice.com
825. Ibid.
826. www.thenation.com
827. www.wsj.com
828. Ibid.
829. www.foreignpolicty.com
830. www.slate.com
831. Ibid.
832. Ibid.
833. Ibid.
834. www.mrc.org
835. Ibid.
836. www.guardian.co.uk
837. www.reuters.com
838. www.politicalhumor.com
839. www.thehill.com
840. www.reuters.com
841. www.thehill.com
842. www.cbsnew.com
843. www.latimes.com
844. Ibid.
845. www.ksdk.com
846. www.whitehousedossier.com; www.hotair.com
847. www.nytimes.com
848. www.lonelyconservative.com
849. www.politicususa.com
850. www.realclearpolitics.com
851. www.talkingpointsmemo.com
852. www.dailymail.co.uk
853. www.thehill.com
854. www.louisvilledem.com
855. www.usnews.com
856. www.rightwingnews.com
857. www.huffingtonpost.com
858. Ibid.
859. www.sfgate.com
860. www.thehill.com
861. www.cnsnews.com
862. www.mlive.com
863. www.huffingtonpost.com; www.chicagoist.com
864. www.theblaze.com
865. www.cnn.com
866. www.politicususa.com
867. www.talkingpointsmem.com

868. www.thejanedough.com
869. www.realclearpolitics.com
870. www.newsbusters.org
871. www.newser.com; www.nytimes.com
872. www.commondreams.org
873. www.bluevirginia.us
874. www.rightwingnews.com
875. www.democrats.com
876. www.rightwingnews.com
877. www.theroot.com
878. www.globalgrind.com
879. www.hufffingtonpost.com
880. www.rightwingnews.com
881. www.washingtonex-aminer.com
882. www.thinkprogress.org
883. www.washingtonpost.com
884. www.thehill.com
885. www.crooksandliars.com
886. www.occupt316.org
887. www.upi.com
888. www.azstarnet.com
889. www.goodreads.com
890. Ibid.
891. www.policallyillus-trated.com
892. www.addictinginfo.com
893. www.notable-quotes.com
894. Ibid.
895. www.msnbc.com
896. www.cbsnews.com
897. www.commondreams.org
898. www.digg.com
899. www.sun-sentinel.com
900. www.dailykos.com
901. www.sun-sentinel.com
902. www.tampabay.com
903. www.latimes.com
904. Ibid.
905. www.huffingtonpost.com
906. www.mediaite.com
907. Ibid.
908. Ibid.
909. www.mediaite.com; www.nationaljournal.com
910. www.mediaite.om
911. www.politicalhumor.com
912. Ibid.
913. Ibid.
914. Ibid.
915. Ibid.
916. Ibid.
917. Ibid.
918. www.urbanlegends.com
919. www.politicalhumor.com
920. www.top10-best.com

921. Ibid.
922. Ibid.
923. Ibid.
924. www.politicalhumor.
     com
925. www.politicalhumor.
     com; www.latimes.com
926. www.politicalhumor.
     com
927. Ibid.
928. www.politico.com
929. www.hecklerspray.com
930. Ibid.
931. www.freethoughtblog.
     com
932. Ibid.
933. www.politicalhumor.
     com
934. Ibid.
935. Ibid.
936. Ibid.
937. Ibid.
938. Ibid.
939. Ibid.
940. Ibid.
941. Ibid.
942. Ibid.
943. Ibid.
944. Ibid.
945. Ibid.
946. www.wsj.com
947. www.politicalhumor.
     com
948. Ibid.
949. Ibid.
950. Ibid.
951. Ibid.
952. Ibid.

953. Ibid.
954. www.huffingtonpost.
     com
955. www.thegrio.com
956. www.theweek.com
957. www.politicalhumor.
     com
958. Ibid.
959. Ibid.
960. Ibid.
961. Ibid.
962. Ibid.
963. Ibid.
964. Ibid.
965. Ibid.
966. Ibid.
967. Ibid.
968. www.democraticun-
     derground.com
969. Ibid.
970. Ibid.
971. www.alternet.org
972. www.dimwittedpoli-
     tics.com
973. www.mustsharejokes.
     com
974. Ibid.
975. Ibid.
976. Ibid.
977. www.rollingstone.com
978. www.huffingtonpost.
     com
979. Ibid.
980. www.selfdeprecate.
     com
981. Ibid.
982. www.politicalhumor.
     com

983. www.selfdeprecate.
com
984. www.hecklerspray.com
985. www.selfdeprecate.
com
986. Ibid.
987. Ibid.
988. Ibid.
989. Ibid.
990. Ibid.
991. Ibid.
992. Ibid.
993. Ibid.
994. Ibid.
995. Ibid.
996. Ibid.
997. Ibid.
998. www.politicalhumor.
com
999. www.selfdeprecate.com
1,000. www.johnboehner.
house.gov
1,001. www.politicalhumor.
com